Elaine

Words to Live and Do

Words to Live and Do

Donald C. Irwin

A Hearthstone Book

Carlton Press Corp. ❖ **New York**

Copyright © 1995 by Donald C. Irwin
ALL RIGHTS RESERVED
Manufactured in the United States of America
ISBN 0-8062-5093-3

They have not been written to be discussed,
but they are words to live and do.

Martin Luther

Contents

Foreword

This book is not necessarily meant for academic theologians, though I would hope some of them might glance at it. It is particularly intended for sincere Christians who are not secure in their understanding of the faith and are willing to take another look at the Bible as the textbook for Christian truth.

These chapters are simply written by intention. I have tried to keep up on theological trends and know the meaning of most of the "sound bite" words. There are critical questions, and I touch on some of them; however, my concern is not to impress but to express. I remember the Apostle Paul's sharing that "the world by wisdom knows not God"; he spoke of "the message about the Cross" as the power and wisdom of God.

I pray that these writings will be affirming rather than polemic. We are told by Peter that we should "always be ready to make a defense . . . for the hope that is in you; yet do it with gentleness and reverence." My spirit in writing is one of peace. Some will quarrel with my observations, but I hope they will not quarrel with the Bible insofar as I am faithful to the text.

I have tried not to be "preachy," but I am not always consistent. It is difficult to break old habits, particularly after having preached over five thousand times.

I am indebted to so very many who have helped me in my faith as they have exposed me to the Scriptures. They include pastor friends, professors, Hebrew scholars, devotional writers, and many Bible teachers. I must mention three sources of help that have given affirmation and fresh insights during the last twenty years: The Bethel Bible Series, which, as I studied and taught it, refreshed the memory of my early years of learning that the Bible has a unified story to tell, and reminded me of the words of an early professor who kept saying, "Think like a Hebrew"; Hans Rookmaaker, the late professor at the Free University of Amsterdam, whose lectures opened up for me in a new way the development of classical humanism into a negative philosophy that has so saturated our western culture, that it has given new relevance to our Christian Gospel; and *The Bible Speaks Again*, a study made by scholars of the Netherlands Reformed Church, which pleads, as does William Barclay in its Foreword, "for the Bible to be given a chance to speak for itself."

The teachings and writings of all of those to whom I owe a debt have so penetrated my thinking that I am not always sure what are their words and what are mine. It is difficult to sort it all out. Some may recognize their words as unacknowledged quotes. I hope they will forgive me any plagiarizing and count it "one of the privileges of the communion of saints." Even that quote cannot be acknowledged. Had I known that I would be writing a book, I would have kept better track of my sources. But I meant no evil; to be labeled a "literary kidnapper or thief" terrifies me.

Some may find the sharing of so many biblical references too bulky. I merely tried to let the Bible speak a lot. You need not be constantly turning pages. The references are there to keep a check on me *and to encourage you in your own Bible study.*

Finally, I have used the New Revised Standard Version translation (unless otherwise noted), because it shows a sensitivity to the generic gender words, and does it with integrity.

My thanks to some very special people: Flo Learned, who edited my first drafts, correcting my grammar, but who also encouraged me to move on. Her critical suggestions were invaluable. Laurie Heermance, my granddaughter, for putting all of this into the computer and preparing it for publication. And Glenn, her husband, who helped. And especially Georgia, my dear wife of fifty-five years, who all those years encouraged me in our ministry and helped me to be faithful to God's Word and to the Lord whom it reveals.

> "To him who loves us and freed us from our sins by
> his blood, and made us to be a kingdom, priests serving
> his God and Father, to him be glory and dominion for-
> ever and ever. Amen."
>
> Revelation 1:4,5

Introduction

As I was nearing the close of my pastoral ministry, I made two decisions: the first, to shred many of the written sermons I had in my "barrel"—I feared that when I passed on someone might read them; the second was to stop defending the Bible and to concentrate on attempting to teach what it says.

I studied to be a minister during the years of the Modernism versus Fundamentalism debate in religious circles. It was a fierce time. On one side there seemed to be a careless, if sometimes sincere, questioning of the integrity of the Bible and what were called fundamental doctrines of the faith: Inspiration of Scripture, the Virgin Birth and Deity of Christ, his Sacrificial Death, his Bodily Resurrection, and others. There was a display of arrogance on the part of some scholars who raised the questions. On the other side, there was an ardent defense of those truths, and we should be grateful for it; however, there developed a dogmatism on the part of some of the defenders that seemed to deny the spirit of Scripture. And it was colored by a kind of separatist legalism. I was blessed as a young searcher to attend a seminary whose teachers ministered to both my mind and my heart. One memory of my first year stands out: Our Hebrew Old Testament professor kept saying, "Gentlemen, you don't know your Bibles."

After World War II, I was called to be the pastor of a church where I remained for twelve years. This was my second blessing. It was a biblically correct church. The people knew their Bibles for they had been taught well by my predecessor. They had a background with some of the great Bible teachers of those years. I loved that church. Some of my readers will know what it means when I say that it was my Ephesus. I had to study my Bible seriously in order to keep up with the people, and to keep enough ahead so they might be challenged.

It was also an outreach-oriented congregation. I was there during the Civil Rights Movement years. The church was located in the center of one of the choicest neighborhoods for social change and at the edge of the Mason-Dixon line. I am grateful to God for this congregation of biblically taught Christians who received, loved, and included into the fellowship people of color. It was not easy to do at that time. One of my emotional thrills came when an African-American lady, who had become a member of our congregation, introduced me to her two friends, who had come to visit her in the hospital, as "my pastor." The experience gave relief from some of my personal guilt. But more than that, for me those years with that fellowship of Christians helped push out the borders of the Gospel.

Martin Luther is reputed to have written, during days of the Reformation, that the words of the Bible "are not written to be discussed but are 'words to live and do.'" This appraisal of Scripture dictates the spirit for these writings of mine.

After a good many years as pastor and teacher, I am concerned that so few Christians know what they are supposed to believe. So many do not know their Bibles. It follows that they don't know what it means to trust God, nor how Christian faith fits into everyday living. They are left without a satisfying experience of the grace of God and the assurance of his provided redemption. That is a tragedy! And if they do not know the "words to live" they will not understand "the words to do." The agenda facing the church today is awesome and demanding, and we ought to be offering something distinctive. My concern is that we may be running out of informed and confident Christians.

Toward the close of his Gospel, John writes: "Now Jesus did many other signs in the presence of his disciples, which are not written in this book; but these are written that you may come to believe that Jesus is the Messiah (Christ), the Son of God, and that through believing you may have life in his name."[1] The life he talks about is eternal life, the good life, to be lived here and now and ultimately beyond the grave. What John shares about his experience with Jesus Christ is for us to believe, and in believing discover life in the richest dimension. John is also concerned that we have *assurance* of the reality of eternal life: 'I write this to *you who believe* in the name of the Son of God, so that you may *know* that you have eternal life."[2]

Likewise, it was the continuing burden of the Apostle Paul that Christians grow and mature in their faith and confidence, so that it becomes evident. For example: "As you therefore have received

Christ Jesus the Lord, continue to live your lives in him, rooted and built up in him and established in the faith, just as you were taught, abounding in thanksgiving."[3]

I once heard the late James E. Stewart ask some members of the clergy, "are we helping Christian people to understand their faith?" He then went on to challenge them: "We must stop thinking of the Bible only in a moralizing way and begin to use it in teaching THE FAITH."

What is meant by "the faith?" Jude speaks of "the faith which was once for all entrusted to the saints."[4] "The faith" is that body of truth found in the Bible about God, humanity, creation, and all that God wants us to know about the meaning of life and history, as he is involved in all of it. We must know the details of "the faith" if we are to be informed Christians and confident in our faith.

Note also that faith includes *trusting* that body of truth. In the Hebrew, the language of the Old Testament, there is a word which is translated both "truth" and "faith." Truth is not simply a theological concept but something to be trusted and acted upon. For example, the Bible declares a great truth: that God has a purpose in all things for the Christian. Christians may say they accept that truth, but how they react when missing a bus or losing a sale indicates how well they know the significance of "the faith."

This book hopes to help us see the Bible as God's living word, which speaks to Christians of truth and assurance so that they can "live and do." Give the Bible a chance to speak for itself.

xiii

Words to Live and Do

1 The Book and Its Words

The Bible is the textbook of our Christian faith, and there is no authentic Christian theology apart from its text. The Apostle Paul tells us why it is so important for us to study our textbook: "All scripture is inspired by God and is useful for teaching, for reproof, for correction, and for training in righteousness, so that everyone who belongs to God may be proficient, equipped for every good work."[1]

Are there questions about the Bible's credibility? Yes, lots of them. Many scholars will tell you the question of the doctrine of inspiration of Scripture is the most difficult to answer. It wasn't until the Reformation that the final decision was made about what books should be included in the Bible we use today, and this raises many questions. An excellent book for tracing the historical development of the Bible and the movements that have challenged its authority and integrity is *The Bible Speaks Again*, the result of an extended study in the mid-sixties by scholars of the Netherlands Reformed Church.[2] This book was a reverent and serious attempt to better understand the Bible. After a review of what was known as Historical Criticism, which began in the 1800s, the Dutch scholars came to this conclusion: "After the first somewhat stormy period, however, it gradually became clear that the Bible has a remarkable tolerance," and they said they more fully appreciated the truth contained in it. The credibility of the Scriptures does not depend upon our having satisfying answers to all our questions. The story in the Bible and its unity are enough to begin to discover what it has to say about our Christian faith. We start our study of it with a confident affirmation that the Bible is the Word of God.

All of my ministry has been in and through a confessional church. This means that we believe certain truths, and in a series of historical creeds we *say* what we believe. It is important to note that what we say is based upon the Bible. For instance, in our vows of ordination, we accept the Scriptures as the "*unique* and *authoritative* witness to Jesus Christ, and God's word to you," and we will "be instructed and led by the confessions"—while declaring that such confessions can and do err. A member of the clergy is ordained to the office "of the *Word* and Sacrament." Therefore, we believe that the Christian faith is founded upon the Bible, the Word of God, and that there is no other *written* source of ultimate truth.

There are many ways in which God reveals himself. Paul speaks of natural revelation: "Ever since the creation of the world his eternal power and divine nature, invisible though they are, have been understood and seen through the things he has made."[3] The Psalmist worships by singing "The heavens are telling the glory of God; and the firmament proclaims his handiwork."[4] The things that God has made tell us much about our creator.

What a revelation comes to us in the *Word made flesh!* We read, "Long ago God spoke to our ancestors in many and various ways by the prophets, but in these last days he has spoken to us by a Son . . . he is the reflection of God's glory and the exact imprint of God's very being."[5] Jesus is the living Word, the ultimate revelation. However, we only learn about Jesus from the written testimony of those who experienced him in the flesh. The Apostles who lived and walked with him gave their testimony in the Gospels. A somewhat contemporary historian, Josephus, mentions Jesus in passing. Later in the first and second centuries others add their testimonies. But the authoritative word about Jesus is the Bible. Thus, the Bible is the Christian's textbook for religious truth and guidance, as well as for assurance and hope.

The Bible is not an easy book to understand. Perhaps we were sold a bill of goods by those who declared that the Reformation gave us an open book that anyone can understand without benefit of teachers. It is not quite that simple. Strange teachings have emerged from some who claim to have found truth that no one else has discovered. The prophets warned about false teachers, and so did Jesus and the Apostles. Much of the questioning of the credibility of the Bible arises as a result of misunderstanding the text. Even though the Bible is the best-selling book in our country, it is suspect among many who have never read or studied it. The suspicion comes not from what the Bible says, but from those who have attempted to tell us what it says. Knowing a little bit of the Bible can be scary. We do need teachers and fortunately God has bestowed the gift of teaching upon certain people in his distribution of spiritual gifts.[6]

There are certain principles that can help us discover what the Bible is saying. First, since the Bible was written to God's people, it *can* be understood by them. It is a Hebrew / Christian book that tells the redemptive story of God's unfolding plan for blessing his people that they might be a blessing to the world. He wants these people—Israel in the Old Testament and Christians in the New Testament—to know and experience the story so that they can share it with others. Without this story, Christians really have nothing unique to say.

There is so much to learn, and well-taught Christian disciples can expand their biblical horizons. Paul prays that God "may give you a spirit of wisdom and revelation as you come to know him (Christ)."[7] He adds this singular truth when writing to the church in Corinth: "What no eye has seen, nor ear heard, nor the human heart conceived, what God has prepared for those who love him—these things God has revealed to us through the Spirit." And he goes on: "Now we have received not the spirit of the world, but the Spirit that is from God, *so that we may understand* the gifts bestowed upon us by God. And we speak of these things in words not taught by human wisdom but taught by the Spirit."[8]

If you are a Christian, the Holy Spirit lives within your heart and mind and can lead you to understand the text of the Bible so as to experience it. Truth comes alive. There is a dynamic to the written word when it is blessed by the Spirit. Paul speaks of the gospel as "the power (literally, "dynamite") of God for salvation."[9] Luther spoke of experiencing the Bible as the book of God who speaks.

A second principle is this: In order to know the blessing of mind and heart you must learn to think like a Hebrew. I can still hear my Old Testament professor say, "Gentlemen, think like a Hebrew!" He kept saying it as he introduced us to the biblical story. Then a few years ago I took a course in preparation for teaching the Bethel

Bible Series, and the author, Harley Swiggum, kept saying, "Think like a Hebrew!"

You see, the Bible was written by Hebrews to Hebrews. The Hebrew people approach the biblical message differently from most of us. Westerners have grown up thinking like Greeks. Our concepts are philosophical, analytical, deductive, and for the most part, in the abstract.We learn in order to comprehend. On the other hand, the authors of the Bible thought of religion in life-human situations. They saw truth in specific, practical details, making much of the *events* of religious experience. They learned in order to reverence and to live. Faith was more meaningful than systematic theology. For example, a Hebrew sings, "The law of the Lord is perfect, reviving the soul; the decrees of the Lord are sure, making wise the simple; the precepts of the Lord are right, rejoicing the heart; the commandment of the Lord is clear, enlightening the eyes."[10] To the Hebrew, the Torah—God's Word—was a way of life, his Good News.

Suppose a sincere Greek-Christian thinker were asked, "What is man's relation to God?" The answer might be: "Man is finite, God is infinite; man is temporal, God is eternal; man is weak, God is almighty." A sincere Hebrew religious thinker might reply: "All of the above but a whole lot more. God creates man and woman for fellowship with himself and each other, for history, for meaning, for living, for events, that they might make a great contribution as God enables them."

Harley Swiggum used this illustration: The first words of the Bible say, "In the beginning God created the heavens and the earth." Now what immediately comes into the Greek-thinking mind? *How* did he do it? But the Hebrew would respond, "That's not the point. God made it all, and he is worthy of our praise." "O Lord, our sovereign, how majestic is your name in all the earth!"[11] Later we read in Genesis that the serpent tempted the man and the woman. The Greek mind wonders: How can a snake talk? The Hebrew says: Sin came into the world as a result of their disobedience and there are dreadful consequences for human history; the evidence: Cain kills his brother, Abel.

A word of caution here: The above need not deny the historicity of the man and the woman or the early chapters of Genesis. It is simply to illustrate that the message is more important to the Hebrew, and if we think like a Hebrew the biblical story will more easily become our story too. A Hebrew approach to the Bible opens up the meaning of life and relationships, those areas in which faith can relate and which are the longings of the human spirit. It helps us to realize that the Bible is not a science book, or a history book, or just another piece of good literature. It is a book about men and women and God.

The drama *Fiddler on the Roof* gives us an insight into Hebrew life and feeling. Remember Tevya in his conversation with God, how he questions the tragic affairs of his life and wants to remind God of this fact. Humorous, yes, but he is a true Hebrew. Think like a Hebrew when you study the Bible.

Thirdly, in order to fully understand the Bible, we need to discover what it is actually saying. That seems obvious, but it is amazing what some people come up with when asked about a particular Bible verse or passage. One of my seminary professors who taught us how to study a scriptural text in order to prepare a sermon, on occasion, after assigning the class a particular passage, would invite one of us to write an outline on the blackboard for discussion. I can still hear him saying, "Mr. Irwin, what you have written may be true, but you didn't get it out of *that* text." It was the best teaching for sermon and lesson preparation I have ever received, and it has kept me captivated and enthused about teaching the Bible throughout the years of my ministry. What does the text say? That is different from what we think of as interpretation or what the text means to me, where our own subjectiveness and personal biases creep in. We need to know what the Bible says before we can interpret what it means. Experience does not authenticate truth; truth authenticates experience. Bible study groups find it difficult to follow this guideline, because they are anxious to get to its meaning. However, if they are to honor God's word, this is where they must begin.

Also, we need to know the meaning of words. I believe that the English dictionary is one of the best commentaries on the Bible. For example, here is the definition of the biblical expression "justification by faith": "the act by which a sinner is free through faith from the penalty of sin and is accepted by God as righteous." That could be right out of the heart of the book of Romans. May I suggest that you use the dictionary yourself for words as sin, faith, savior, propitiation, and prodigal.

The derivation of words is also interesting and helpful. Take the word "sacrifice"; you will discover that it derives from two Latin words which mean "to make sacred." If we use the word in the most common meaning, "to give up something," what could a modern American Christian, surrounded by so many things, possibly give up in order to make a sacrifice? But using the basic meaning of the word could say a lot about Christian commitment. Mark Twain is credited with the remark: "The difference between the right word and the almost right word is the difference between lightning and a lightning bug."

Thus, we must try to discover what the authors meant by a particular word. Blessed by the Holy Spirit, they wrote out of their own experience with God. David tells it differently than Isaiah; Matthew than John; Paul than Peter. The message is consistent, but each adds a personal dimension to the story. That is why we can relate to it, but we need to know what the words say in order to experience the blessing. Those writers intended that their readers should understand what they wrote.

What about context? It has been said that a text taken out of context is a pretext. There are those who flit around the Bible like spiritual hummingbirds looking for saccharine in verses they interpret as God's special message for them, without any regard for the context. That can lead to false hope and even false teaching. The context matters. How often have you heard the biblical expression, "A little child shall lead them," to emphasize reaching adults for commitment to Christ or for some other noble cause? But note the context of the expression, where the prophet, Isaiah, is talking about the Messianic Age, when the "wolf shall live with the lamb, the leopard shall lie down with the kid, the calf and the lion and the fatling together, and a little child shall lead them."[12] No real harm is done, but the use of the expression is taken out of the intended context.

The *immediate* context is important. For example, Jesus tells the parable of the Prodigal Son, a precious story about the wayward son who returns home and is accepted without condition by his father.[13] It mirrors the heavenly Father's grace. However, note the immediate context with which the lesson begins: "Now all the tax collectors and sinners were coming near to listen to him. And the Pharisees and the Scribes were grumbling and saying, 'This fellow welcomes sinners and eats with them.' So he told them this parable. . . ."[14] The emphasis of the parables of the lost sheep, the lost coin, and the lost son was to expose the bigotry and prejudice of the contemporary religious leaders. Another example: one sect has used a verse in Proverbs, "The Lord created me at the beginning of his work, the first of his acts long ago,"[15] as a proof-text that Jesus was a created being and not one who shares eternity with God the Father. However, the immediate context shows that the writer, using a poetic form of personification, was talking about wisdom and not about Jesus.

Then there is the context of the entire Bible. Any single passage of Scripture is a part of the whole. A core verse is John 3:16: "God so loved the world that he gave his only son, so that everyone who believes in him may not perish but may have eternal life." Many Christians know that verse by heart, and in a sense it sums up the reason for Christ coming into the world. But we need to ask: Who is God? What is the meaning of love? Who is the son? Who is everyone? What is the meaning of believe, perish, eternal life? The answers to such questions can only be found within the context of the entire Bible if we want to know the blessings of this great text. We learn from the Old Testament that God is Yahweh, Lord, Creator, called Father and sometimes acting like Mother, Giver of the law, Covenant Maker and Keeper, Author of redemptive history—it is *he* who gave his son. And that is only scratching the surface. Answers to the other questions can be discovered by bringing the context of the whole Bible to this verse. Think of an inverted pyramid with the apex resting on the verse. Into the pyramid is crowded all that the Bible has to say about it.

Next in our study we must recognize the differences in culture, language, and philosophy of the various times in which the inspired writers lived. We call this the "cultural context" of the Bible. The authors were writing, not as stenographers, but out of their own experience with God. Each of them lived in a particular time and place. Hebrew culture was different from Roman and Greek and was influenced by both of them. The New Testament world was alive with philosophies strange to Israel. Paul writes a letter to the church at Colossae against the background of gnosticism, a system of thought then current about the problem of good and evil, which had crept into the church as a heresy concerning the person of Jesus Christ. This does not mean that what the writers said has no relevance for us who live in the twentieth century; rather, each of them gives singular dimensions to the truth shared. It is important to note that the laws and guidelines in the Book of Leviticus, designed for better relationships with one another and given to a large community of people spending forty years in the desert under a kind of martial law, should not necessarily guide our lives. A seeker after biblical guidance must carefully note the cultural context of some of the things Paul wrote to the Christians living in the pagan and immoral city of Corinth. He talks about people not marrying and women not cutting their hair, and numerous other accommodations of a cultural nature.[16] We need to come to the Bible with literary and historical understanding if we are to be true to the integrity of Scripture.

Today, words are often reported out of context to discredit a person's integrity. In a similar way the Bible has been discredited by those who lift verses out of context. Most of the uninformed critics of the Bible find their problems not with the Bible itself but with misrepresentation of what the Bible is saying. They have been aided by those who use Scripture for some cause by declaring that the Bible supports it, when nothing could be further from the truth.

In summary: We can turn to no other book to find the definitions of our Christian faith in its inspiration. There are no other documents contemporary with the happenings of the biblical records that teach Christian truth. Thus, if we want to know about God's way with Israel and the Church, if we want to know about Jesus Christ and his meaning for the world, we have only the Bible as a reference. If the four evangelists—Matthew, Mark, Luke, and John—were wrong, we cannot now hope to make it right. It has been said, "Unless we accept their testimony, the Jesus of history is lost forever." The only Savior we know is the Christ of the Bible.

The authentic view of Scripture is an attitude rather than a doctrine. It is not known by what we say about it, but by what we do with it. The sincere follower of Jesus will love this book—not worship it, but love it. It will be studied diligently, believed and carefully obeyed. When a person comes to faith in Jesus Christ, the Bible becomes a necessity. The real blessing comes when the Spirit of God bears testimony to the Word of God in the believer's heart. One of the first evidences of a converted experience is the new-found hunger for the Word—not to dissect or build up a doctrinal system, but to satisfy a desire to know God.

An old friend of mine wrote, "Any rational person who is willing to pay the price can discover and learn to appreciate the Bible as a body of literature, a record of history, a book of theology, or as a mine of sermonic texts and quotable words. But something more than brains is required if one is to discover that the Bible 'is a lamp to his path.' It is the heart, not the head, that sings, 'O how I love thy law; it is my meditation all day long.' "[17]

The Bible *is* the Christians textbook. Approach your study of it not for research but in a devotional quest for meaning, asking the Holy Spirit to enlighten you. It is a living book, just waiting for you to become acquainted with it.

When one ceases to quarrel with the Bible and reverently seeks to learn from it, there is blessing and guidance to be found, for it talks confidently about the meaning of life and death, sin and forgiveness, the dignity of mankind, social responsibility, peace of heart and mind, love, the tragedy of materialism, the graces of living, sexual joy and sexual exploitation, family life, healthy patriotism, personal integrity, hope, feminism, true religion, teenage wisdom, the outcome of history, the Middle East—and much about God's coming into the world in the person of Jesus Christ. What more could you possibly want from a book?

2 God Tells His Story

This chapter begins with a look at biblical theology. "Theology" is a good word, though not one used in the Bible. It is a combination of two Greek words: *theos*, meaning God, and *logia*, coming from a root word meaning collection. Tracing the development of the word, theology means the collection of all we can discover about God, while using reason and wisdom to do so. It is the study of God with the added dimension of application of truth to life. *Biblical* theology means that what we discover rests on what we find in the Bible about God—truth that is inherent in the Bible itself. This leads to three observations.

First, biblical theology *begins with God*. So much of theology today is undertaken by sociologists, ecologists, psychologists, and socioscientists who begin with men and women in their human situation. We are indebted to the many who share the realities of the human predicament and work diligently to find answers. But their conclusions are not necessarily consistent with biblical findings. To some, God is not a part of the answer to the human situation; answers will be found as humans relate properly to one another and to their environment. Others may agree that God can prompt men and women to moral commitment, but this approach tells us little about God or about the true nature of men and women.

Biblical theology is a *theology of revelation* and begins with God sharing truth about himself. A good point to remember: the content of the Bible is not primarily about theology but about God. Most people have at least a vague idea of a god, but that idea may be far from the Christian biblical revelation concerning the true God. Many religions arrive at their beliefs about a god by observing nature, linking it to the forces evident for their survival; others by examining the human mind and emotions, searching for him within themselves. Then there are those who would eliminate God completely. The Christian faith begins with the God who is revealed in the Bible.

Certainly biblical theology does not refer to God without relating him to the human situation or the created universe, else what would be the sense? Christians are theists. They believe the one true God created everything in the universe and continues to be intimately involved in all the details of that creation—including especially man and woman created in his own image. We call this providence, described as God's attention concentrated everywhere.

The Book of Genesis begins with the story of creation. God made the heavens and the earth, and then made man and woman "in his image, in the image of God he created them; male and female he created them."[1] In just twenty-five verses the story of the creation of the universe is told, but when the man and woman appear, history begins! The human story becomes the reason for creation. God's interest in mankind is what the Bible is all about. Biblical theology is the study of God *and* his relation to the universe he created, but it *begins* with the God of the Bible, not the human situation.

A second observation: Biblical theology is *more than doctrine*. It is not a denial of doctrine, but more than doctrine.

Another type of the study of God is "systematic theology," which is a gathering together of what all of Scripture plus philosophy and other disciplines have to say about God and his relation to humanity and the universe. It is a *reasoning toward* God. The result of this systematic approach is doctrine, another good word and valuable in helping Christians avoid falling prey to the peddlers of false religion. Paul writes to Timothy and Titus about sound (healthy) doctrine. However, to some that means dogma, which they associate with being dogmatic. This is where biblical theology helps us, because it is not an exercise in the abstract; it relates truth to life for blessing and guidance. Paul describes a behavior consistent with sound doctrine: "For the grace of God has appeared, bringing salvation to all, training us to renounce impiety and worldly passions, and in the present age to live lives that are self-controlled, upright, and godly."[2]

You will note in Paul's letter to the churches that after dwelling on some profound teachings (doctrines), he always follows with extensive reminders about the ways Christians are to respond to such revelations of God's grace. For example, the first eleven chapters of Romans share a large body of truth about "justification by faith" with its many implications. Then he writes, "I appeal to you, *therefore*, brothers and sisters, by the mercies of God, to present your bodies as a living sacrifice."[3] The next four chapters share the practical application of truth consistent with a response to the earlier teaching of the book.

Doctrine is not for doctrine's sake; there must always be a transition from theology to Christian behavior. Doctrine defines duty; truth falls within the context of morality. Nothing is as dead as dead orthodoxy.

In the Bible we discover that many of the teachings about God do not show up as doctrines, but are in the context of what should be our response. We read: "God's love was revealed among us in this way: God sent his only Son into the world, so that we might live through him. In this is love, not that we loved God but that he loved us and sent his Son to be the atoning sacrifice for our sins." Amazing, divine love! But note the following verse: "Beloved, since God loved us so much, we also ought to love one another."[4] Thus, there is more than doctrine in the message of the Bible.

A third observation: Biblical theology *puts truth in the context of a story*. A few years ago while traveling in Israel and on a boat crossing the Sea of Galilee from Tiberius to Capernaum, our young Jewish guide asked me why our people were so interested in the *places* of Palestine—Bethlehem, Nazareth, Jerusalem, Jericho, etc. I told him I thought it was because these are the places where it all happened—where Abraham and Sarah, Moses and David, Mary and Jesus lived out their events. Ours is a faith that is tied to history, about things that took place. It all adds up to a story that was acted out, and the land is important because it is the theater of the redemptive story.

The expression "it came to pass" occurs thousands of times in the Old Testament, and at least one hundred times in the New Testament. It comes from a word in the Greek language that means "becoming," as though something is in the process of movement. The Bible tells a story, and it is always moving from one saving event to another in a history that is constantly unfolding.

The more you study the Bible, the more you are captivated with its emphasis upon the *events* of the story it tells. God speaks to us through events. The Hebrew word for event is also the one for "word." It is where the abstract becomes concrete. Someone has commented that in the Old Testament "history provided a creed, a recital of the great acts of God to which Hebrew people could respond in faith for the present and for the future." How often God would say to Israel, "I am the God of Abraham, of Isaac, and of Jacob," and the people would remember their ancestors. The story was always alive in the covenant memories of God's people. In their worship they would sing the great providential songs, rehearsing the details of God's moving among them. In Exodus we read: "I am the LORD, your God, who brought you out of the land of Egypt, out of the house of slavery; you shall have no other gods before me...."[5] It was the Exodus event that not only gave authority to God's will for the moral life of his people, but also a sense of their destiny. They had been redeemed in order to be a blessing.

Then there came the greatest event of all, the event of Jesus Christ—his incarnation, his ministry, his death, his resurrection. What a story—when God spoke in sending his Son! God loves the world, so he sends his Son to redeem it. Truth comes alive in the event. There is a strong relationship between what is being heard and what is happening. Jesus *talks* about compassion, then goes about doing good, healing, shedding tears, meeting people where they are. To position-seeking disciples he talks about true greatness, then he calls a little child and sets him in their midst and says, "Unless you . . . become like children, you will never enter the kingdom of heaven."[6] Jesus talks about religious hypocrisy and then points to a poor widow putting two small copper coins into the temple treasury and says, "This poor widow has put in more than all those who are contributing . . . she out of her poverty has put in everything she had."[7] That is the way the story is told in both Testaments. The story resides in our Christian memories also.

Finally, the biblical story declares that God is involved in our world of space and time. Commenting on the current interest in "Narrative Theology," Alister McGrath in his article "The Biography of God" wrote: "Often systematic theology creates the impression that God is presented to us with a set of ideas, as if revelation were some kind of data bank," and adds: "The Gospel is not primarily a set of ethical principles; it is about the affect of an encounter with God on the lives of individuals and the history of nations."[8]

That indeed is the essence of biblical theology; it tells a story about real life in a real world—our world.

Sadly, many Christians do not know the Bible's story. They have learned the Bible piecemeal in Sunday School, as though it were merely a collection of short stories about heroism and moral platitudes. They have heard about David and Goliath, Joseph and his coat of many colors, Jonah and the big fish, and they have lost the impact of *the* story in the events of the story. For example, consider the story of Jonah, an exciting enough tale about God's deliverance to cause children to listen intently when effectively told. But it is a part of a larger story about Israel's responsibility to be a "light to the nations," and their refusal to fulfill it.

From the time of the early church until the present there have been efforts to allegorize the events of Scripture—to search for symbolic meanings behind the happenings. Allegory as a figure of speech is employed a great deal in the Bible. To illustrate his teachings, Jesus spoke of the Good Shepherd and his sheep, the Vine and the Branches, and so on. The allegories, parables, and other symbols are used throughout Scripture not to mystify but to make clear. No one needs to be initiated in order to have the insider's "key" for understanding. Yet, there are some who teach that it is the symbolism and not the event that is important. Sometimes they use the word "myth."

For example, a vital part of biblical teaching does use Jesus' death on the cross as a model for a Christian's commitment to humility, to laying down one's life for others or for a cause, or to bearing the burden of unjust suffering. The Bible talks often about these lessons from the cross. However, it is possible to so allegorize the event of the cross as to miss the larger story about God's final solution to mankind's sin and guilt in sending his Son to bear the curse of their sins, to offer forgiveness upon the price paid, and to open up the possibility of a new life for the believer. The redemptive story began in Eden and reaches its climax at Calvary.

Biblical theology emphasizes the full story, a story that begins with God revealing himself to us.

3 The Story Told

The biblical story is real history, yet the Bible is not primarily a history book. Its purpose is always religious and its concern is chiefly the revealed love and redeeming grace of God worked out in history.

The story begins with God creating the universe and then creating the man and the woman in his image to dwell on the earth, while making abundant provision for them to live the good life. Thus, history begins. The man and woman rebel. They sin and fail and so mar the image they cannot recover their dignity. This is known as the Fall. The man and woman are estranged from each other and from nature. Guilt follows. This is the tragic story of mankind throughout the whole of history. In the choice they have made to disobey God they are helpless and hopeless. Jesus would later describe them as "sheep without a shepherd."

The heart of the biblical story begins when God provides a loving way to restore the man and woman, and this becomes the message of the remainder of the Bible. God chooses a people, Israel, to be the objects of his special redeeming love and a channel of blessing to all mankind. We pick up the story in Genesis: "Now the LORD said to Abram, go from your country . . . to the land that I will show you. I will make of you a great nation, and I will bless you, and make your name great, so that you *will be a blessing* . . . and in you all the families of the earth shall be blessed."[1] Thus were born the Hebrews, later to be known as the People of Israel, God's Chosen People. For centuries Israel remained a witness to the blessing of what it means to worship and serve the one true living God, a recipient and purveyor of divine truth, and a channel through whom the Messiah would come. Israel was truly *blessed to be a blessing*.

In 1949, on the first anniversary of the establishment of the nation of Israel, I heard Abba Eben, the first Israeli Ambassador to the United States, say: "I offer no apology for the three thousand square miles history has given my people, because it is Israel which has saved the mind and the soul of mankind from heathenism." He was repeating the biblical story from the Old Testament.

The Old Testament is the record of the redemptive purpose of God as it unfolds in the history of a chosen people and culminates in the coming of the Messiah. Many times the nation of Israel strayed from its purpose. The Prophets reminded them of their peculiar place in the purpose of God and kept calling them back. They warned of judgment for disobedience, but also told of the restoring mercy and love of their God. Some of the books of the Old Testament (Ruth, Esther, Job, Psalms, Ecclesiastes, and Lamentations) tell the experience of those who felt the movement of God's purpose in their lives.

Throughout the Old Testament story there is a consistent relationship between the great truths (doctrines) about God and his ways with mankind. There are three basic questions that are constantly being answered in the narrative: What is God like? What are the man and woman like? What does God require of human beings? Flowing from the answers to these questions we discover what God was doing and continues to do.

As you read and study the Old Testament you have a feeling that something more is coming, there is a mood of expectancy. The prophecies concerning God's purpose as given to Abraham and his descendants are left unfulfilled. The return from the Babylonian captivity has lost its excitement. The promised Messiah has not come, and the hope of his coming has dwindled. Soon you realize that New Testament history does not follow immediately upon Old Testament history, which closes with the Persians ruling the world. The New Testament shows the Romans ruling, and there is evidence of the influence of another people, the Greeks. There are groups of religious people, such as the Pharisees, Sadducees, Zealots, and

Herodians, who are not mentioned in the Old Testament. Keep in mind, a period of four hundred years has elapsed between the two testaments. We are indebted to historical scholars, both sacred and secular, who have researched the records that tell of the interval. Some of the books of the Apocrypha, found in the Roman Catholic Bible, are helpful in tracing the history of the period.

When the story continues in the New Testament, it centers around the person of Jesus Christ. He is the long-awaited Messiah (not recognized by most of his own people), the Redeemer, God's final Word to mankind. Mary gives birth to her firstborn son in a manger in Bethlehem, and she and her husband, Joseph, call his name Jesus. This was history's finest hour! The Apostle Paul puts it this way: "Jesus Christ, the Son of God, whom Silvanus, Timothy and I have preached to you, is himself no doubtful quantity; he is the divine Yes. Every promise of God finds its affirmative in him, and through him can be said the final Amen, to the glory of God."[2]

Jesus is born at a certain time in a certain place, in Bethlehem of Judea (a part of Palestine). It is during the rule of the Roman Emperor, Augustus, and while Herod is king of Judea and Quirinius governor of Syria. These are persons of traceable first century history; thus, Jesus was born into history and into geography.

Jesus lived thirty-three years in Palestine, the son of a carpenter, Joseph. We have no record of the eighteen years after the age of twelve, but at age thirty, he began a three-year crash ministry of teaching, working miracles, "and going about doing good." He chose a company of twelve disciples whom he taught and trained, especially in preparation for continuing his ministry after he would leave. At he height of his career, he was murdered on a cross, but rose from the grave and ascended into heaven, promising to return. This is the history recorded in the Gospels of Matthew, Mark, Luke, and John.

There is a chronological history in the New Testament, but the significance of the record in the Gospels is centered in the question: Who is Jesus Christ? The importance of the correct answer to this question is given by John: "These are written so that you may come to believe that Jesus is the Messiah (Christ), the Son of God, that through believing, you may have life in his name."[3]

The story continues. After the resurrection of Christ, the disciples and other believers, endowed with special power by the Holy Spirit, engage in a ministry that begins in Jerusalem and Judea and spreads throughout Samaria to the north. They are joined by a man named Saul (Paul), who is chosen by God to be "an apostle to the nations."

Paul becomes the dominant missionary in the subsequent history of the New Testament, and carries the message concerning Jesus Christ to all Asia Minor (Turkey), Greece, and finally to the capital city of the empire—Rome. He establishes churches in each city, and they become instruments for continuing witness and service to the rest of mankind. This is the history recorded in the Book of Acts, which closes open-ended. Paul, John, Peter, and Jude write letters of encouragement, interpretation, correction, and advice to the churches and their leaders. These are the New Testament Epistles.

The New Testament closes with the Book of Revelation, a treatise of rich imagery, given to the church going through intense persecution for its witness to Jesus Christ. Christians are encouraged with visions of the exalted Christ, declared to be Lord of Lords and King of Kings, whose Kingdom will never end. God will triumph over evil, and God will close out history in a way that will vindicate his people. Jesus Christ is the key to that history.

That is the New Testament part of the story, but the significance of the Acts and Epistles is centered in the question: What is the Church? The answer declares that the Church is the New Israel, "God's chosen and peculiar people."[4] They are a people of destiny, and like Israel, are entrusted with a mission that will bless the world. They are to bear witness to what God is doing through Jesus Christ, and having experienced him in their lives, they are to be instruments of God's loving concern for all mankind. Love dictates that concern. They are empowered by the Holy Spirit and instructed by the Apostles. They are one in Jesus Christ and matured by discipline. They are blessed with all spiritual blessings and entrusted with the news of the boundless riches of Christ. They are a select people with a triumphant, engaging future—not a people by accident.

This is the biblical story encapsulated. The details are worked out in the lives of the people of the Old and New Testaments, and the story continues in the secular history that follows. Many years ago a book entitled *The New Acts of The Apostles* developed a church history that began in the time of the Apostles and moved into the twentieth century. The joyful news is that the story of God's redeeming love revealed ultimately in Jesus Christ and attested to in the Bible is still alive in his Church today.

4 He Is!

Our Christian faith begins with the God who reveals himself in the Bible. Who is he? A. W. Tozer said, "What comes into our minds when we think about God is the most important thing about us." The important question of religion is not, Is there a God? but What is he like?

The apostle Paul rejoiced when he heard that the believers in the church at Thessalonica had "turned to God from idols, to serve a living and true God."[1] While he was in Athens, he was deeply troubled that the city was full of idols, and when he was invited by the intellectuals of the city to speak to them, this is what he said: "Athenians, I see how extremely religious you are in every way. For as I went through the city and looked carefully at the objects of your worship, I found among them an altar with the inscription, 'To an unknown god.' What therefore you worship as unknown, this I proclaim to you. The God who made the world and everything in it, he who is lord of heaven and earth, does not live in shrines made by human hands . . . in him we live and move and have our being. . . ."[2]

The Bible is not concerned with proving that there is a God, but in affirming the blessings of knowing him. It also exposes the emptiness and tragedy of all false gods that vie for our allegiance. The

Bible speaks of knowing the true God, the one who gives "to all mortals life and breath and all things," in an intimate and authentic relationship. He is the God we "feel after."

The essence of idolatry is the entertainment of thoughts about God that are not worthy of him. In the Bible, both the Hebrew and Greek words meaning "Idol" come from a form of the word "to see"; thus, an idol is the "thing seen." It works like this: a person has an idea about what God is like. Conforming to that idea, he fashions an object that he can see and then worships that object, the product of his own reasoning and imagination. All one needs to be an idolator is to entertain thoughts about God that are not worthy of him.

Jeremiah describes the futility and tragedy of such idolatry: "For the customs of the peoples are false; a tree from the forest is cut down, and worked with an ax by the hands of an artisan; people deck it with silver and gold; they fasten it with hammer and nails so that it cannot move. Their idols are like scarecrows in a cucumber field. . . ." Then he says to God's people who have been tempted to follow the pagan gods: "Do not be afraid of them, for they cannot do evil, nor is it in them to do good. There is none like you, O LORD, you are great and your name is great in might."[3]

Years ago I accompanied a missionary on a visit to a primitive village in southern Sudan where we met a young woman who had returned to her village to have her first baby. She was in severe pain and was sitting beside a dead tree; at its base were meat and meal offerings placed there by a witch doctor. These offerings were intended to appease the wrath of the beneficent god who supposedly lived in the tree, and who would drive out the evil spirit within the girl so the pain would leave. The superstitious fear was evident among the villagers who watched, and we witnessed the hopelessness and tragedy of their idolatry. My missionary friend embraced the girl and told her that the pain she was going through was quite natural. She went on to share the truth about God, whom she need not fear, and the story of Jesus, a name beginning to be known in the village.

At a time when Israel was drifting from God and "playing the harlot" with the gods of the neighboring pagan nations, Isaiah pleaded with his people: "To whom then will you liken God, or what likeness compare with him? An idol? . . . Have you not known? Have you not heard? The LORD is the everlasting God, the Creator of the ends of the earth. He does not faint or grow weary; his understanding is unsearchable. He gives power to the faint, and strengthens the powerless. Even youths will faint and be weary, and the young will fall exhausted; but those who wait for the LORD shall renew their strength, they shall mount up with wings like eagles, they shall run and not be weary, they shall walk and not be faint."[4]

What is God like? He teaches us about himself in the Bible, not in abstract principles, but in living situations. He is a living being—here, there, and everywhere. The Bible is not a dictionary of theology or philosophy, but reveals a living God. In the great faith chapter in Hebrews we are told, "Without faith it is impossible to please God, for whoever would approach God must believe that *he exists* (that he is)."[5]

The significant passage of Scripture that introduces us to the God of the Bible is found in Exodus. The nation of Israel has been in Egypt four hundred years. God has chosen Moses to lead his people out of slavery and back to Palestine where they are to discover who they are—a great nation destined to fulfill the promises made to Abraham. Moses is hesitant and questions his qualifications for such leadership. God promises to be with him, to which Moses replies, "If I come to the Israelites and say to them, 'The God of your ancestors has sent me to you' and they ask me, 'What is his name?' what shall I say to them?" God answered, "I AM WHO I AM" and added, "Thus you shall say to the Israelites, 'I AM has sent me to you . . . the LORD, the God of your ancestors, the God of Abraham, the God of Isaac, and the God of Jacob, has sent me to you'; this is my name forever, and this my title for all generations."[6]

God links himself to history. The presence of God lives on in the covenant memories and hopes of the great figures of Israel's history and their descendants, but much more is found in the expression, I AM WHO I AM. The Hebrew word for "I am" is YAHWEH, used often as YAWE. In English translation, it is LORD in capital letters. Another word, "Adonai," in lower case letters, is used for God, but YAWE is the big word that tells of the God of the Bible.

While the Israelites had been captive in Egypt, they certainly would have been influenced by the Egyptians who worshipped their chief god, RA, the sun god, who was to them the author of life, light, and fertility. During times of doubt and confusion, Israel would have been exposed to Egyptians bowing before pagan images in a system of idolatrous worship. Now they are traveling with Moses to the land of Canaan where there will be hundreds of other deities in centers of worship and life of the nations surrounding them. The images of Baal, Asteroth, and a host of strange gods would always be a temptation to God's chosen people as they dwelled in a pagan land. About to begin new adventures of destiny, they needed to know who they were and who was their one true God.

Through Moses God tells them that he is a reality—I AM, I exist. I always have been and always will be. Here is a living God, not the result of the imagination of humans nor an ethereal "blob" out there somewhere. He finds the cause of his existence within himself. He is a personal being; not a concept of the mind, but a companion of the heart. The Psalmist said it this way: "The LORD is my shepherd, I shall not want,"[7] and "as a deer longs for flowing streams, so my soul . . . thirsts for God, for the living God."[8]

Some translate the I AM WHO I AM designation to mean "He who causes to happen causes to happen," indicating that YAWE is the subject of the continuing biblical story. He motivates history and moves it onward to the great event of the coming of Jesus Christ. YAWE causes it to happen—then, now, and forever.

The first part of this chapter talks about the reality of the one true and living God. Let us look now at the truth that God is the creator and ruler of the universe, who is known to us by revelation. Remember, Christians are theists, and there is a significant difference between theism and deism. The latter describes a god, perhaps the true God, who created a universe and its natural laws but is now withdrawn from it all—like a person making a clock with the power to run and then merely sitting back and observing it unwind. It pictures God as the victim of his own creation and as one who is indifferent to the helpless creatures of the earth. Fate is the word deists use, and they work hard to master it, or they resign themselves to the inevitable.

Theists, on the other hand, believe in YAWE who is revealed in the Bible as creator and ruler of all he has created—he who causes it to happen causes it to happen. In one of the great providential Psalms, the songwriter praises God: "O LORD, how manifold are your works! In wisdom you have made them all; the earth is full of your creatures. Yonder is the sea, great and wide. Creeping things innumerable are there, living things both small and great. . . . These all look to you to give them their food in due season."[9]

The God of the Bible created a universe, and wherever you look in the world you see his creative hand. Everything is interrelated. God made it and he maintains control of it—the stars in their courses, the affairs of the nations, the hairs of your head. He upholds all things by the word of his power. The biblical writers knew that.

The Prophets and Apostles were always calling the people to trust the God of creation and providence. Though they did not know all the details, they knew that God was at work directing Old Testament history toward the coming of the Savior, and New Testament history toward the completion of his ultimate purpose—a redeemed creation! They knew that God did not always move in straight lines, that history would surprise us, thus calling us to faith. But they also knew that God would "gather up all things in him (Christ), things in heaven and things on earth . . . according to the purpose of him who accomplishes all things according to his council and will."[10]

Just as when a stone is thrown into a pond it creates concentric circles that ultimately extend to the farthest shore, so the EVENT of Jesus Christ would affect the whole of history and bring it to its triumphant climax. In Handel's *Messiah*, we sing "Alleluia, for the Lord God omnipotent reigneth." The song, together with the passage in Revelation from which it comes, echoes the biblical record that God is the Lord who motivates and enriches history.

The God of the Bible is the Lord of the Church, just as he was YAWE of Israel. When Paul speaks of the purpose of God being fulfilled, he triumphantly relates: "In Christ we have also obtained an inheritance, having been destined according to the purpose of him who accomplishes all things according to his council and will, so that we, who were the first to set our hope on Christ, might live for the praise of his glory."[11]

The Bible does not attempt to give us a definition of God—it is interested in our getting to know him. However, it does *describe* him in various ways, usually within the context of his dealings with mankind. Many attributes were ascribed to him, but in the visions of himself given to us, the one that stands out is his divine and infinite *holiness.* In Exodus, we are told the story of Moses leading Israel out of Egypt under the favor of God's direction. Shortly after they had crossed the Red Sea on dry land, Moses and the people sang a song. It is the language of a redeemed people celebrating in worthy praise him who has given them their freedom. They said, "The LORD is my strength and my might, and he has become my salvation; this is my God, and I will praise him, my father's God, and I will exalt him . . . Who is like you, O LORD, among the gods? Who is like you, *majestic in holiness,* awesome in splendor, doing wonders?" [12] Majestic in holiness! It is the same quality of God in the vision of Isaiah which caused him to cry, "Holy, holy, holy is the LORD of hosts; the whole earth is full of his glory."[13]

The root meaning of the word "holy" is "to set apart, to put at a distance." It is used with regard to sacred vessels set apart from common use to be employed in worship. It describes our God in his distinctiveness, as completely "other" than the objects of pagan worship. Through the prophet, Isaiah, who continues to speak of the creative and providential acts of YAWE, God says: "To whom will you liken me and make me equal and compare me, as though we were alike?"[14]

Holiness is the singular attribute that seems to gather together all the other descriptive qualities that are part of God's intrinsic nature: his perfect righteousness and moral purity, his infinite love, mercy, truth, justice, goodness, and wisdom. These set him apart and call for a difference in the quality of living on the part of those who would be his people. So he says to Israel, "I am the LORD your God; sanctify yourselves therefore, and be holy, for I am holy."[15] And Peter echoes, "Like obedient children, do not be conformed to the desires that you formerly had in ignorance. Instead, as he who called you is holy, be holy yourselves in all your conduct."[16]

Today we seem to have lost this understanding of God. It is gone from the popular mind, and very largely from the mind of the Church. God's holiness has caused some sinful people to tremble. Isaiah said, "Woe is me! I am lost, for I am a man of unclean lips, and I live among a people of unclean lips."[17] Job said, "I despise myself, and repent in dust and ashes."[18] But where do you find that kind of coming to God today? Without it, our worship becomes formal and sometimes an insult, and we have lost our feeling for morality. Plato said, "The divine nature is the fountain of all virtue." For us the will of God is grounded in his infinite perfection, his holiness. Only a revelation of God like that will ever convince men and women of their own sinfulness and helplessness, and their need for the *full* demonstration of God's nature—his mercy and love. There is renewal with the Lord! That is the Good News, but moral integrity must start with a sound understanding of who God is.

We discover God somewhere in the tension between the remoteness of God and the closeness of God. Moses sang, "Who is like you, O LORD . . . Who is like you, majestic in holiness, awesome in splendor, doing wonders?" Isaiah saw the Lord high and lifted up. Yet the Psalmist said, "The LORD is my shepherd, I shall not want." The New Testament speaks of God as a "consuming fire," and Jesus bids us call him "Father." Every sincere Christian knows the tension. Isaiah helps us here when he writes: "For thus says the high and lofty one who inhabits eternity, whose name is Holy: I dwell in the high and holy place *and also with those who are contrite and humble in spirit,* to revive the spirit of the humble and to revive the heart of the contrite."[19]

We are at the heart of the biblical message of God's redeeming love. From the time of the Fall, the God of creative and purposeful history has been reaching for and calling sinful men and women to bring them back into fellowship with himself. It begins in the Old Testament and climaxes in the death and resurrection of Jesus Christ. It is he who breaks the tension and brings God, who seems so far away, near enough to believers for them to call him "Father."

What should be the response of Christians who believe in such a God? It begins with devotion like that found in the Hebrew Shema: "Hear, O Israel: The LORD is our God, the LORD alone. You shall love the LORD your God with all your heart, and with all your soul, and with all your might."[20] This is the theme that occurs many times in the Old and New Testaments, and depicts the honor, loyalty, love, trust, and worship that are due the Lord.

The tragedy of human history began with men and women who did not honor God. In Romans we read: " . . . though they knew God, they did not honor him as God or give thanks to him . . . they exchanged the glory of the immortal God for images resembling a mortal human being or birds or four-footed animals or reptiles. They did not see fit to acknowledge God." And God "gave them up"[21] to their sinful selves. A low view of God is the cause of thousands of other evils.

The way to biblical health begins with worship. "Bless the LORD, O my soul, and all this is within me, bless his holy name. Bless the LORD, O my soul, and do not forget all his benefits—who forgives all your iniquity, who heals all your diseases, who redeems your life from the Pit, who crowns you with steadfast love and mercy, who satisfies you with good as long as you live so that your youth is renewed like the eagle's"[22] sang the Psalmist as he stretched his spirit in praise for such a God.

Remember: What comes into our minds when we think about God is the most important thing about us.

5 The Last Word

"The fact of Christ persists." "The three short years of the active life of Christ have done more to regenerate and soften mankind than all the dispositions of philosophers and arguments of moralists." "The name of Jesus is ploughed into the history of the world." "We are dealing with an incalculable personality." "Apart from Christ I find I have no hold on God at all." These are some of the statements made by historians, authors, and others, and they are of one accord in saying that there is something singularly unique about this Person—Jesus Christ.

That he lived, died, and rose again are facts that any thinking person has to consider. But what makes him different from all other religious personages? Our resources for knowledge concerning him are quite limited, so if you want to learn about Jesus Christ, you will need to read the New Testament. There have been no new revelations about him.

Jesus Christ transcends a book, he is greater than that. He is in truth the Word of God! However, in order to claim credible Christian experience, you must know the Jesus of the Bible. Those who were eyewitnesses, or close associates, are the recorders of the Jesus story. The Apostle John talks about "what we have heard, what we have seen with our eyes, what we have looked at and touched with our hands. . . ."[1] That makes him, and the others who shared his testimony, credible witnesses and the story they tell believable. What does the Bible say about Jesus? Who is he?

First, he is part of the biblical story. The Old Testament leaves us looking for something more, something dramatic, something hopeful—an event that would give some answers. And then it happened.: "When the fullness of time had come, God sent his son, born of a woman. . . ."[2] And the world has never been the same!

The New Testament introduces us to Jesus as a *person in history*. He is not a myth, nor is there anything mysterious about him—incalculable, yes, but not a part of the occult. As we shall see, in him we encounter God, we are in the presence of the Eternal. Jesus was no figment of the imagination, he really did walk in Palestine. He entered history as certainly as Cyrus the Great, Caesar, or Socrates. Born at a certain place and in a certain time, his mother was Mary, his father Joseph. The genealogies of Matthew and Luke trace his human roots to historical families who are part of the Old Testament story.

He was raised in Nazareth where "the child grew and became strong, filled with wisdom; and the favor of God was upon him."[3] He was in the temple in Jerusalem at the age of twelve, after which "Jesus increased in wisdom and in years, and in divine and human favor."[4] At about age thirty, he appears at the Jordan River to be baptized by John the Baptist, and heard the voice from heaven, "You are my Son, the Beloved, with you I am well pleased."[5]

Thus began a ministry of teaching, healing, showing mercy, and working miracles which took him all over Palestine. At the age of thirty-three, he was crucified in Jerusalem but was resurrected and ascended into heaven. That is the biblical and historical record of the EVENT of Jesus' coming into the world. God was acting, and continues to act, through an historical person. Our Christian faith is more than ideals of hope, love, joy, peace, and good will, all a part of our witness; it is confidence in a Person who lived, died and rose again to be our Savior and to impel us to give substance to our ideals. Christianity is not based on experience but on the reality of history.

As noted before, biblical religion is unique in its stress on history. Other religions tend to look for God in nature (the world about us), or in mystic experience (the world within us). In contrast, Christianity is the story of things that happened in history from Abraham to Jesus Christ. "If nobody knew that it happened, no one could be a Christian."[6] It is important to believe that Jesus passed our way, as the Bible tells it. Christianity is not merely a religion; it is based on the unique self-disclosure of the one, true, living God in personal and historical terms.

The Gospel story tells us about a Person known in Nazareth and Palestine as Jesus, the son of a carpenter. However, if we stop here we fall short of the fuller manifestation of the Person. The significance of the record is centered in the deeper revelation of the question: Who is Jesus?

Jesus goes beyond historical limits while still a part of history. Jesus did not begin with Bethlehem—he predates creation! The Apostle John guides us to the deeper meaning of Jesus: "In the beginning was the Word, and the Word was with God, and the Word *was* God. *He* was in the beginning with God. All things came into being through him, and without him not one thing came into being. . . . And the *Word became flesh* and lived among us, and we have seen his glory, the glory as of a father's only Son, full of grace and truth."[7]

While in Africa some years ago, I was discussing our faith with a Muslim sheik. When I shared the truth of God coming in the person of Jesus, he shook his head in bewilderment and then said, "I wish our religion had something like that." It seems to me that this is the great miracle. The Virgin Birth of Jesus ought not surprise us or be a stumbling block, if God was really taking human form. This is called the Incarnation, literally the "enfleshment" of God. It is not a word used in the Bible, but the truth is embodied in the testimony that "the Word became flesh and lived among us." The evidence abounds through the Gospels that *God* stepped into history and geography. This is where we discover that Jesus parts company with all other religious figures. He *is* unique.

It is understandable that when people are confronted with the truth of the Incarnation they often go into a kind of intellectual tailspin, for we are faced with a paradox, an apparent contradiction. However, there are some things that are beyond the grasp of human logic. The divine-human nature of the Redeemer is one of these truths. Someone said, "Such a truth had to be revealed; no one could have imagined it." It helps to "think like a Hebrew," but I must again emphasize that the truth about the personality of Jesus comes directly from the Bible. People may quarrel with the idea, but the biblical truth is evident.

The testimony of the Apostles concerning the uniqueness of Jesus was constantly being challenged by the Greek thinkers of their day, some of whom found their way into the Church. It led to such affirmations as that of Paul: "He is the image of the invisible God, the firstborn of all creation; for in him all things in heaven and on earth were created, things visible and invisible, whether thrones or dominions or rulers or powers—all things have been created through him and for him. He himself is before all things and in him all things hold together. . . . For in him all the fullness of God was pleased to dwell, and through him God was pleased to reconcile to himself all things, whether on earth or in heaven, by making peace through the blood of his cross."[8] And finally, "For in him the whole fullness of deity dwells bodily."[9]

Jesus is the object of our faith, not simply the example of our faith. Nowhere in the New Testament is the word "faith" or "belief" used of Jesus; such words belong to those who put their trust in him. What does this revelation about Jesus mean?

First, it tells us that God speaks to us the ultimate Word. "Long ago God spoke to our ancestors in many and various ways by the prophets, but in these last days he *has spoken to us by a Son*. . . . He is the reflection of God's glory and the exact imprint of God's very being, and he sustains all things by his powerful word."[10] God has always had something to say, and now he has really said it: "The WORD became flesh."

Suppose you have a pen pal living in a distant place whom you have never met. Letters are sent back and forth between you, and from them you learn much about this new friend—personality, interests, talents, etc. One day in the mail you receive a handmade gift that reveals more and adds to your knowledge and respect. Later there is an opportunity for a visit in person! This is a simple illustration, but it resembles God's speaking to us. His written word faithfully tells us much about himself and his purpose. The things he has created in our universe tell of his eternal power and glory, and we are awed by it. But then he came into the world, and we learn what God is really like. When we see Jesus, we see God!

On one occasion in the Gospels, Philip said to Jesus, "Lord, show us the Father and we will be satisfied." Jesus said to him, "Have I been with you all this time, Philip, and you still do not know me? Whoever has seen me has seen the Father."[11] Like most of us, Philip was struggling to comprehend God, for no one has seen him. Like Philip, we have ideas about God, pictures in our minds, and most of us see him existing in some form. These ideas probably arise from our psychology shaped by our relationships. But none of these pictures really satisfies until we see God revealed in Jesus, and we begin to understand and believe and are satisfied.

It is interesting to note that in John where it states that Jesus has "...made God known,"[12] the verb comes from a word that is translated as "exegeted." This literally means to "draw out from," and pictures a person pulling out of a word everything that word has to give up in meaning. Thus, Jesus has "exegeted" God. Follow him through the Gospels and learn what God is like: His acts of mercy, his power over the elements, his wisdom, his grace, his concern for mankind, his insistence on justice, and ultimately his love at Calvary. The one sufficient revelation of God is Jesus Christ, the WORD of God incarnate. Redemptive love becomes very personal in Jesus, and it takes place in history.

In the Old Testament, Israel heard the message of God's redemptive love and became aware of it in many of their events. The Psalmist wrote "I acknowledged my sin to you, and I did not hide my iniquity; I said, 'I will confess my transgressions to the Lord,' and you forgave the guilt of my sin."[13] He knew God's love and experienced it. But then Jesus appears and redemptive love is made clear in a Person. He demonstrates it over and over again in his ministry, and he acts it out while paying sin's price on the cross. Paul says that God proved his love for us when Christ died for us while we were sinners.[14] John puts it this way: "God's love was revealed among us in this way: God sent his only Son into the world so that we might live through him. In this is love, not that we loved God, but that he loved us and sent his Son to be the atoning sacrifice for our sins."[15]

There are many blessings that flow from the Incarnation. When Jesus was born, he was called "Emmanuel," which means "God with us."[16] He brought God so very close. I like the story about the Christian mother who enjoyed teaching her little daughter lessons of faith and trust. One summer evening after prayers, she tucked the little girl in bed, put out the light and went downstairs. An electrical storm came rolling out of the west with vivid flashes of lightning and a reverberating roar of thunder. Suddenly, there was a simultaneous blinding flash and a deafening crash, and when the echoes died away the mother heard her daughter calling desperately for her. She found the little girl in tears and trembling, and after soothing her for a few moments she said, "Hasn't mother told you you need never be afraid because God is always with you?" The girl responded by putting her arms around her mother's neck and saying, 'Yes, Mama, but when the lightning and thunder are so awful, I want someone near me what's got skin on."

I think we can reverently say that Jesus is God with "skin on," near enough to be understood and experienced. We are told in Hebrews that Jesus was tested just as we have been and is therefore able to sympathize with us as we face the realities of life.[17] He has been through it all, experiencing temptation, sorrow, fatigue, distress, thirst, hunger, rejection, loneliness, pain, and suffering, and all the emotions common to humans. He understands and brings a caring God near to us. It is Jesus who breaks the tension between the remoteness and the closeness of God.

This truth leads us to another step in the wonder of the Incarnation. Coming into the world as a man, Jesus was equipped to be our Redeemer. In the Book of Hebrews we are introduced to the theme of the preeminence of Jesus Christ, largely spelled out against the background of the Hebrew sacrificial approach to God and his blessing, all of which prefigured the atoning work of Christ. We could summarize the message of the book by saying that without Christ you cannot get beyond the shadow of God. Then we read, "And it is by God's will that we have been sanctified through the offering of the *body* of Jesus Christ once for all."[18] Peter echoes this truth: "He himself bore our sins in his *body* on the cross, so that, free from sins, we might live for righteousness; by his wounds you have been healed."[19] God "prepared a *body*" to take away our sins![20]

God's plan for creation's deliverance from futility and release from sin begins to unfold in a manger in Bethlehem. The baby in the manger will grow in stature, and as a man will walk the roads of Palestine, doing and saying all that we read in the Gospels. What a blessedness we see in that noble Person; what lessons we learn from his superb teachings, what stirrings are ours as we watch the displays of his compassion. But one day he set his face resolutely toward Jerusalem where he would die. That is why he came in that body. His mother, Mary, sensed the destiny when she and Joseph took their baby boy to the temple for blessing and heard the devout Simeon say, "a sword will pierce your own soul too."[21] The cross was the destiny of the Redeemer—*that body was made to die!*

There is a tendency to bypass this central theme of the Gospels. We like to celebrate Christmas and hurry on to Easter; we don't like to spend too much time on Good Friday. There you have to deal with sin and inhumanity—and creation's tragedy. It is not a pretty sight at Calvary. There are no brass-covered crosses, but a rugged cross made of two rough pieces of wood. There is sweat and blood when Jesus bears our sins in his own body. Then there is that piercing cry, "My God, my God, why have you forsaken me?"[22]

There must have been more than physical suffering at that awful place. Paul tells us that Christ became a curse for us,[23] and adds that though he was without sin, he "was made sin for our sakes."[24] Could it be that Jesus was vicariously experiencing the devastating condemnation due us when he bore our sins on the cross as he "tasted death" for men and women? Who can really understand sin's price? God had to take sin seriously and dealt with it in his Son, whom he sent to die for us. God makes no easy offer of salvation. Jesus had to get as low as we were in order to bring us to safety—all made possible by the Incarnation. Paul sums it up best when he speaks of Jesus Christ "who, though he was in the form of God, did not regard equality with God as something to be exploited, but emptied himself, taking the form of a slave, being born in human likeness. And being found in human form, he humbled himself and became obedient to the point of death—even death on a cross.[25]

By the way, as we see so often in Paul's writings, the great teachings are found within the context, not as doctrines but as examples for our living response. In this instance he is begging Christians to show compassion, sympathy, love, and humility, and leads into the above passage by saying "Let this same mind be in you that was in Christ Jesus." The humiliation and love-death of Jesus became not only the inspiration for our Christian concern for mercy, justice, and love deeds, but also the dynamic. With no profound theology of the cross, there is no impulse to true righteousness. Today, when a suffering world is demanding the best Christian response, it will take more than a few gentle words or a vague feeling of love (or a scolding) to follow Jesus. Love alone, the love born at Calvary, will transform us from do-gooders to Christian activists.

When we think of the uniqueness of the Incarnation, we must remember that it is *God* in human form who hangs on the cross. "He died upon a cross of wood and made the hill on which it stood." A truly great mystery, but that is the heart of the story the Bible tells. "In Christ *God* was reconciling the world to himself.[26] It is a *revealed* mystery tucked away in the inexhaustible wisdom and loving plan of God. Our response cannot even attempt to explain it. Our response can only be *faith!*

What was it that changed Saul (Paul) from a man on his way to Damascus to round up followers of Jesus to be persecuted to a man suddenly proclaiming that Christ was the Son of God? I believe that the answer is found in the Damascus Road experience.[27] When Saul was stricken by a light form heaven and heard a voice saying, "Saul, Saul why do you persecute me?" he replied, "Who are you, Lord?"

As a Hebrew, the only Lord Saul knew was YAWE, the one and only God. Yet he was absolutely certain that the light came from YAWE, and that the voice came from him also. When the answer came, "I am *Jesus* whom you are persecuting," the impact was enormous. Jesus is YAWE, the God of my forefathers! It was this disclosure that changed Saul into the apostle whose ministry ultimately took him to the capital of the empire.

Once we can grasp by faith that *God* died for our sins, we will never be the same. It is too overwhelming. "So if anyone is in Christ, there is a new creation: everything old has passed away; see, everything has become new! All this is from God, who reconciled us to himself through Christ, and has given us the ministry of reconciliation." [28]

Remember: he was given the name "Jesus," a form of the Old Testament "Joshua," which means Savior, because he was to "save his people from their sins." [29] His death on the cross accomplished it; his resurrection attested to it.

There is yet another impact to the Incarnation. Jesus shows us what men and women are intended to be and what they can become. As *God* in human form he shows us what God is like; as God in *human form* he shows us what men and women are like. Review the Genesis account of creation, where God is said to have made them *in his image:* rational beings who can think and manage the domain entrusted to them; emotional beings who can love and be loved; moral beings who can respond and weigh values, having minds, memories, and wills. They were created to be creative, like God; they would delight in doing good, like their Creator. They were pristine people in a pristine environment. Then, through their disobedience, sin entered, and the man and woman tragically lost their capacity to be what God had intended them to be. The image lost its luster.

But the resounding message of the New Testament is: the potential of man and woman *in Christ.* He is the supreme model for each of us. Carlyle called him the "Proper Man." Milton said, "Our humanity is at this moment high-enthroned above all heights." In Jesus of Nazareth, true humanity was realized once for all. That the Son of God should become the Son of Man is the highest tribute God could make to humanity. The Incarnation was a glorification of all that is properly human.

Jesus has shown what we ought to be. You have heard the expression, "To err is human." It is nothing of the sort. Jesus was without sin, yet he was perfectly human. Sin is an aberration of what is truly human. Jesus stands in history as the True Human. He came to demonstrate what we ought to be, and for us to accept the present condition of man and woman portrayed in our newspapers and on TV screens as the picture of humanity as God meant it to be is an insult to God and to Jesus. Men and women wallowing in aberrant behavior, exploiting one another, cheating, lying, degrading by bigotry, belittling—all described by Paul as "works of the flesh"—is not what God had in mind.

Jesus is a protest to all that is inhuman, and he is the bright light pointing to what we can become. Through Jesus, God shows us that we are redeemable. He came to make us whole (the Greek word "save" means not only to rescue but especially to "make whole"). His death on the cross was a vicarious suffering for our sins, and it provided the dynamic for making us complete. He died to make us human! Christianity is not a religion. It is concerned about human culture and demonstrates it in Christ, where love is love, beauty is beauty, truth is truth, righteousness is righteousness, reality is reality, service is service.

The believer begins by knowing Christ as Savior and Redeemer. Then God starts the process of molding, shaping, and transforming us into the image of the true human, Jesus Christ. The evidence is seen in what Paul calls the "fruit of the Spirit, love, joy, peace, patience, kindness, generosity, faithfulness, gentleness and self-control,"[30] the very graces that adorned Jesus. That's truly human!

There is a parallel truth here: Jesus in human form shows us the worth and dignity of every man, woman, and child, and is a protest to every kind of exploitation of human beings. The identification of Jesus with mankind is so very real that he could say, when ministering to those in need: "Truly, I tell you, just as you did it to one of these, my brothers, you did it to me."[31] He declares his identity with every person, regardless of race, class or culture. Amazing! The implications are vital and decisive to our Christian commitment to bring people to know him as Savior and Lord so that they may find fulfillment in him and then follow him in his loving ministry to the needy ones.

It makes a tremendous difference whether you view humans as the result of natural forces or as the creation of God in his image. The two views are directly opposed to one another. The latter is Christian and biblical, and therefore the view that lifts man and woman it to a dignity described in the Genesis account of creation. This dignity is celebrated in Psalm 8, and expressed nobly in Jesus Christ. As a man, Jesus identifies with all of us and declares that the Divine Original, though obscured by sin, is in every person whether redeemed or not. Sin does not destroy humanness. "He is the potential bearer of a crown, even though he may gamble it away a thousand times."[32]

Early in my ministry, I felt frustrated when asked to preside at the funeral of a person who not only gave no evidence of being a Christian believer, but whose life was one of ill repute. But as I matured biblically, I realized that this person was created in the image of God and was one with whom Jesus identified in his coming. I remembered that there was a dignity to every human being, and though a person had grieved his Maker, he was one for whom Christ died. The Incarnation declares that everyone be treated with compassion, and that includes a decent burial.

The social implications are intense for the disciple of Jesus. As a Christian, I cannot be indifferent to what is happening to people. During the Civil Rights uprising in the fifties, I recall a southern man saying "I like the *status quo*, but I am also a Christian." The Incarnation pushes us into the arena of human events and needs, not as bystanders, but as participants with an attitude of protest against all that is dehumanizing. What the prophets had to say about justice and mercy became embodied in Jesus. He traveled the countryside doing good, and his very presence, as well as his teachings, was an exposure of all forms of bigotry, hatred, indifference, and human exploitation. The Lord Jesus, when he saw the multitudes harassed and helpless, as sheep without a shepherd, less than what they could be, was moved with compassion. He identified with their suffering, and it led to his death.

Jesus, who bears the perfect image of God, bears also the perfect image of man and woman. As we are being transformed by God's grace into his image, we had best be with him, not simply in church on Sundays, but "where cross the crowded ways of life," where human life and need happen.

There is something about the name—JESUS! Earlier reference was made to the Philippian Epistle where Paul tells of the humiliation of Jesus. Though he shared equality with God, he emptied himself, became a man and died a criminal's death on a cross. These words follow: "Therefore God also highly exalted him and gave him the name that is above every name, so that at the *name of Jesus* every knee should bend, in heaven and on earth and under the earth, and every tongue should confess that Jesus is Lord, to the glory of God the Father."[33]

What a name! What a Person who bears that name! Lives have

been changed by that wonderful name. Remember the thief on the cross next to Jesus? He knew that he was justly condemned, but Jesus had done nothing to deserve this scene. He turned and said, "*Jesus*, remember me when you come into your kingdom." That was all the theology he knew, that somehow Jesus was the answer to his deepest need. But it was enough for Jesus to reply, "Truly I tell you, today you will be with me in Paradise." [34] Max Lucado observes, "I smile when I think of a grinning ex-con walking the golden streets who knows more about grace than a thousand theologians."

Then there is the story of Philip's encounter with the Ethiopian ruler on the road from Jerusalem to Gaza. The young man was resting in his chariot and reading the Old Testament book of Isaiah. Philip approached him and was invited up into the chariot to interpret the passage he was reading. The record says, "Then Philip began to speak, and starting with this Scripture he proclaimed to him the good news about Jesus."[35](He literally gospeled him with Jesus). It was enough for the Ethiopian; he asked to be baptized!

What a transforming name! The contemporary religious leaders had trouble with Jesus' claim that he was "the Christ" and were angered with his claim that he was "the Lord," but they discovered that the people flocked to him as "Jesus"; they heard and found some good news in him. It is the evangelical and evangelistic name!

But it is also the *exalted* name. Jesus is the name he bore throughout his lifetime on earth, through the cross, through the resurrection and the ascension. The disciples were gathered with Jesus to receive his commission to be his witnesses to the "ends of the earth," when suddenly he was lifted up into a cloud. The disciples were gazing up in bewilderment when the announcement came: "This Jesus, who has been taken up from you into heaven, will come in the same way as you saw him go into heaven."[36]

Jesus is the name he bears now in his priestly ministry. It is his glorified name. We get only glimpses of this part of the story in the Gospels, for they give the record of his coming in "humiliation" to be our Savior. In the transfiguration, [37] for a brief moment Peter, James, and John were given the privilege of witnessing his glory. Jesus tells of his coming in glory, and Apostles wrote of it and, the Book of Revelation, in spectacular imagery (telling of the triumph of his kingdom), offers the honor that is due his name, when "every knee shall bow and every tongue confess that he is Lord." Here is one scene: "Then I looked, and I heard the voice of many angels surrounding the throne and the living creatures and the elders; they numbered myriads of myriads and thousands and thousands, singing with full voice, 'Worthy is the Lamb that was slaughtered to receive power and wealth and wisdom and might and honor and glory and blessing!' Then I heard every creature in heaven and on earth and under the earth and in the sea, and all that is in them, singing. 'To the one seated on the throne and to the Lamb be blessing and honor and glory and might forever and ever!' And the four living creatures said, 'Amen!' And the elders fell down and worshipped."[38] Later there were loud voices in heaven saying, "The kingdom of the world has become the kingdom of our Lord and of his Messiah, and he will reign forever and ever."[39]

Remarkable! That simple name of Jesus, borne by the One who is the KEY to history.

Years ago, a friend of mine met a Muslim commissioner in India who was fingering a string of beads that he called "the golden cord that binds my soul to Allah." They were "gems of glory," "jewels of joy," "pearls of Paradise." Each bead stood for one of the ninety-nine sacred names of Allah. Upon his return home, my friend was prompted to look for the names of Christ in the Bible. He found two-hundred and noted that they began with "Jesus" (" . . . for he shall save his people from their sins") and ended with "Jesus" (at that name "every knee shall bow").

Is it any wonder that the writer of the Book of Hebrews encouraged a persecuted people in the first century to "consider Jesus who is the apostle and high priest of our confession?"[40]

GOD HAS SPOKEN!

6 The Gospel Simply Told

The word gospel means "good news or tidings." It comes from a word translated "evangel," which in its purest definition tells about God's grace manifested and pledged in Christ.

Good news can come in many ways to people in different circumstances. For example, what is good news to persons suffering from physical hunger? Of course the answer is the promise of food immediately. What is good news to a jobless person, one who has cancer, parents who have lost a child, one experiencing racial abuse? The answers are obvious and are found in the Bible, which is full of this kind of good news God's people are called to share.

Jesus began his ministry with this announcement: "The Spirit of the Lord is upon me, because he has anointed me to bring *good news* to the poor. He has sent me to proclaim release to the captives and recovery of sight to the blind, to let the oppressed go ·free."[1] He stated that his coming was the fulfillment of the prophecy of Isaiah,[2] and in that context his ministry was very definitely concerned with the physical needs of people. The Bible has much to say in calling us to a social gospel—a ministry in behalf of those who suffer deprivation, injustice, bigotry, abuse, indifference—those conditions that are the tragedies of so many lives.

My emphasis here is the Gospel *according to the Apostles* who wrote the four gospels, and the New Testament writers who enlarged upon the meaning of those recorded events about Jesus Christ. Remember, our textbook for Christian truth is the Bible.

There is a singular gospel that the Apostles talk about, which is the true "evangel." It is the *good news of salvation through Jesus Christ!* It is definite, precise, clearly stated, and accepted by the Apostles as the greatest proclamation God could make to mankind. The promise began in the creation story. After sin entered our history, God told of a deliverer who would rescue us from sin's predicament. It was the hope of Old Testament history, and comes to its reality in the event of Jesus. That is why the New Testament books of Matthew, Mark, Luke, and John are called "the Gospels."

Through the life, death, and resurrection of Jesus Christ there is forgiveness of sin, restored relationship with God, abundant life, wholeness, and an impulse to live with integrity. Listen to the Apostle Peter: "Blessed be the God and Father of our Lord Jesus Christ! By his great mercy he has given us a new birth into a living hope through the resurrection of Jesus Christ from the dead, and into an inheritance that is imperishable, undefiled, and unfading, kept in heaven for you who are being protected by the power of God through faith for a salvation ready to be revealed in the last time."[3] That's Good News!

The Apostles were obsessed with this particular emphasis of the gospel. They believed passionately that no one could ever earn the love of God and, therefore, were totally dependent upon his grace revealed in Jesus Christ. Paul speaks of having been "set apart" for the gospel of God when he was called to be an apostle.[4] He claimed that he received the truth of the gospel by revelation from God.[5] He suffered extensively "in defense and confirmation of the gospel," and what was happening to him "has actually helped to spread the gospel."[6] Near the close of his ministry he said: "I do not count my life of any value to myself, if only I may finish my course and the ministry that I received from the Lord Jesus, to testify to the good news of God's grace."[7]

There is no question about what gospel Paul is committed to. In writing to the Galatian Christians he is astonished that some of them were "turning to a different gospel," which he declares is a perversion of the gospel of Christ "who gave himself for our sins to set us free from the present age, according to the will of our God and Father."[8] Note carefully that the Apostle is not defending a theological dogma, but is passionately concerned that his readers are confused, and instead of knowing the assurance of the gospel are questioning their faith, which in turn leads to suspect morality.[9] Note also that Paul's emphasis is not a distinction between the "social gospel" and the "personal gospel"; both are biblical. Rather, it is a distortion of the Gospel of Grace in Jesus Christ.

There is no such thing as a *simple* gospel. There is no simplicity to the letter Paul wrote to the church in Rome in which we find the gospel exhaustively defined. A professor of mine described the book of Romans as "logic on fire." However, it is possible to trace an outline of the first chapters of Romans and discover the core substance of the "gospel of God, which he promised beforehand through his prophets in the holy scriptures, the gospel concerning his Son . . . Jesus Christ our Lord."[10] Paul makes no apologies for sharing that gospel, which he describes as "the power of God for salvation to everyone who has faith."[11] The dramatic emphasis on *this* gospel is spread throughout the New Testament writings.

There *is* a gospel simply told. We begin with the bad news, which Paul sums up by declaring "*all have sinned* and fall short of the glory of God."[12] According to the Bible, what is sin? It is variously described as transgression of the law of God, literally overstepping the limits; unrighteousness or failure to do what is right at all times; lawlessness, opposition to the law or contempt of it; failure, error, and so on. But the one word about sin that is dominant in the Bible means "to miss the mark." The picture is of a target, with the bullseye the perfect law and requirements of God, or the perfect living out of those by Jesus. In our sinful condition, we fall short and miss the mark of measuring up to God's requirements, or of following the exemplary life of Jesus. We are sinners by omission as well as commission.

Paul goes on to say that *we have shut God out of our lives*, have not given him the honor due him, or shown our gratitude for his benevolence toward us. As a result we have surrendered ourselves to our baser attitudes and emotions, "the lusts of our hearts to impurity," "degrading passions" that lead us to shameless acts, and minds literally stuffed with every kind of wickedness, evil, covetousness, malice, filled with envy, murder, strife, deceit, and craftiness.[13] These are the sins common today, and what you can expect when human nature is estranged from the God of creation who has revealed his power and benevolence in the things that he has made.

Some will react by saying that that may be the picture of the heathen, but surely not of those who have a religious and moral heritage. Paul responds: "You have no excuse, whoever you are, when you judge others; for in passing judgment on another you condemn yourself, because you, the judge, are doing the very same things."[14] And religious rites are of no value in themselves.[15] The answer: "What then, are we any better off? No, not at all; for we have already charged that all, both Jews (those with religious heritage) and Greeks (pagans), are under the power of sin, as it is written: 'There is no one who is righteous, not even one. . . .' "[16]

The last reference says that we are all *under the power of sin.* How often have we said, "The spirit is willing, but the flesh is weak," and with Paul: "I can will what is right, but I cannot do it. For I do not do the good I want, but the evil I do not want is what I do."[17] When teaching young people, I often ask, "Is a person a thief because he steals, or does he steal because he is a thief?" How would you answer? Jesus said: "It is from within, from the human heart, that evil intentions come: fornication, theft, murder, adultery, avarice, wickedness, deceit, licentiousness, envy, slander, pride, folly. All these evil things come from within, and they defile a person."[18] All of this would seem to say that we sin because we are sinners. Our basic problem is not our sins, but our condition as sinners.

Bad news, true, but there is more. The penalty for sin: *"The wages of sin is death."*[19] In the context of the Bible, death has been expressed as the misery of the soul, because of sin, which begins on earth but lasts and increases after the death of the body. This penalty is expressed precisely three times by Paul, when he says that "God *gave them up* to the lusts of their hearts to impurity, to degrading passions, to a debased mind."[20] God abandoned them to themselves, and what vile creatures men and women are when left to themselves. Read the passage which is the context of the above tragic announcement as it spells out the misery of men and women who have left God out of their lives. Claiming to be wise, they become fools; they insult their bodies, which are the expression of their personalities, in allowing their passions to degrade their personhood; they are called reprobate, doing things that are not decent. The marks are vivid indeed—tragedy, misery, *living death*—the seeds of which are in each of us. They are the revelations of our media and are experienced daily by many who do not know God's grace. It is the ultimate alienation that does not end even with physical death.

Also *we are held accountable* for our sins and sinfulness. Paul speaks of the "wrath of God," which means that God stands opposed to our disobedience and punishes the sinner. This concept is hard for us to accept and, in our sentimental idealism, we want to reject it. It is an alarming and terrifying phrase, but there it is![21]

Remember that God's wrath is always tempered by the cross where it intersects with God's mercy. That is the Good News! But in order to experience the wonder of the good news, we must understand that "righteousness and *justice* are the foundation of (God's) throne."[22] Justice is described as equal administration of the law. It guarantees the rights of all, to do right by them, and to mete out fair judgment upon those who deserve it. We respect our justice system and approve of the civil judge who punishes the violator in order to protect the innocent. Because God is God and is characteristically holy, he must deal with sin. We tend not to take sin seriously, but God must, because it is present in the structure of the universe. When Amos said "Let justice roll down like waters, and righteousness like an overflowing stream,"[23] he was defining morality as God defines it. God's moral law is designed for health and happiness of those who were created in his image, and violators must bear a penalty for their disobedience. The Bible declares that the whole world is held accountable to God,[24] and none of us is without excuse.[25]

But wait, there is more bad news. *We are helpless* to overcome our sin and its penalty! The presumed way for men and women to escape from their predicament of sin would be to attempt to keep God's law, by good deeds, or by religious expression and rites, in order to please God and get right with him. But Paul says: "No human being will be justified in his sight by deeds prescribed by the law, for through the law comes the knowledge of sin."[26] It is the law that points out our sin, as it shows us what God requires. It is like a mirror into which we look to see the dirt on our faces, but having seen the dirt we do not use the mirror to remove it. So the law, though perfect, simply exposes and judges our sin, and because of our sinfulness we cannot fulfill the law's demands. The religious leaders of Paul's and Jesus' day possessed the law, but it did not make them keepers of the law. The law is good, but we are not good enough; by ourselves, we are without hope.

Most of us want to pass over this part of the gospel story. We find it extremely difficult to accept this as a description of our state before God. It is often the tendency of the financially, the socially, and the culturally secure to think of themselves as above the "common" sinners. Gross sins are often excused because of the prestige factor. We also have a problem with the "gentle" sins. We have equated immorality only with sex for so long that we have missed what morality is. We struggle with the old piety, which condemns the sins of the flesh and violence, but gives lighter weight to the subtle sins. One has said, "A sinner is one who because of his sin has lost the capacity to know what sin is." The Bible says, "If we say that we have no sin, we deceive ourselves, and the truth is not in us."[27] WE NEED A SAVIOR!

That brings us to the best news of all—*God has provided a Savior for us!* This great announcement comes in Romans 3:21–26, but it is echoed through all the New Testament letters. Let us begin with the preceding verse: "No human being will be justified in his sight by deeds prescribed by the law. But now, apart from the law, the righteousness of God has been disclosed . . . the righteousness of God through faith in Jesus Christ." The "but now" is the greatest phrase in the Bible; it declares the climax of God's plan for redeeming mankind. The language of this passage of Scripture is cumbersome and involved, so I share a paraphrase of the heart of the meaning: "God puts people right through their faith in Jesus Christ. God does this to all who believe in Christ, because there is no difference at all, everyone has sinned and is far away from God's saving presence. But by the free gift of God's grace all are put right with him through Jesus Christ, who sets us free. God offered him so that by his death he should become the means by which everyone's sins are forgiven through faith in him."

Within their context there are at least twenty profound truths in these few verses, but I lift out the few that can lead us to the assurance of the gospel. First, God offered Jesus as a sacrifice of atonement by his blood, which means that by his death every claim that sin and the law have against us is totally paid for, so that nothing need stand between us and our God. In his sacrifice, Jesus assumed our death, and God's holy wrath was satisfied. Our sins are forgiven and we are made right (justified) with God. Literally our sins are picked up and removed from us "as far as the east is from the west."[28] There is no greater proclamation than that God really does forgive sin! "What happiness for those whose guilt has been forgiven! What joys when sins are covered over! What relief for those who have confessed their sins and God has cleared the record."[29] Have you ever said "I'm sorry" and experienced the forgiveness of a friend, mother, spouse? If not, maybe you'll never know the richness of God's forgiveness, but if you have, then you would have to multiply it by infinity to know the blessing of God's grace.

We are redeemed! By the death of Christ we are *set free!* This is another spiritual gift. Contrary to our idealism, we are not "born free." Jesus said, "Everyone who commits sin is a slave to sin."[30] It takes a thousand different forms—bondage to fear, bondage of self, to others, to circumstances, to death, to habits—but most of all to sin and the guilt it places on us. The search for freedom is universal. It is the motivation for every religious feeling, so much so that it is difficult to separate the profane from the sacred. Men and women need freedom from sin's hold on them; it is sin that binds, hurts, destroys, brings fear, frustration, and weakness, and even fear in the search for freedom.

The gospel announces that we can be "free indeed." "Redemption" is a market-place word from Roman and Greek culture, perhaps best explained by an illustration from the slave market of the earlier days in our own country. A slave was placed on the auction block, and buyers bid as they would for any other piece of property. Finally one was declared the highest bidder. He paid the price required for ownership and then unexpectedly turned to the slave and said "Now you may go free." That's redemption. Jesus came not merely to enlighten, to elevate, to model, to influence, to teach. He came to *redeem*, to "give his life as a ransom for many."[31] "Christ redeemed us from the curse of the law by becoming a curse for us—for it is written, 'cursed is everyone who hangs on a tree.' "[32] He gave himself for us to redeem us from all iniquity."[33] He *died* to set us free. This is no cheap redemption, and the freedom cannot be purchased, it is beyond measure.

Paul speaks of the glorious liberty of the children of God. Freedom from sin's penalty: free to be God's people, to serve others in love. "And because you are children, God has sent the Spirit of his Son into our hearts, crying 'Abba! Father!' So you are no longer a slave, but a child, and if a child then an heir through God."[34]

There is much more. Paul says that it will take the ages to come for God to show the "immeasurable riches of his grace in kindness toward us in Christ Jesus."[35] But how can we experience all that he has for us? By the *free gift of God's grace!* Grace is the big word, meaning his unearned favor toward men and women, his love and mercy toward the undeserving. "Christ died for the ungodly . . . God proves his love for us in that while we still were sinners Christ died for us."[36] And remarkably it comes to us as a free gift! One works for wages, but receives a free gift by simply saying thank you.

We receive the blessing *through faith*. God does this to all who believe in Jesus Christ. "Faith" and "believe" are the same word in the Bible, the former the noun, the latter the verb. Faith is difficult to define; it is something like "feeling it in your bones." Basically, it is a response to God's matchless favor, the acceptance of his gracious bounty. Yet we are not called to blind faith; there must be content. "Faith comes from what is heard, and what is heard comes through the word of Christ."[37] Faith is not an irrational leap into the dark. We are to believe certain facts— the facts told by the gospel. Then we must be persuaded by the facts, and agreeing to them assent to their truth. What is that truth? Jesus really did come to do the things that he did in order to accomplish our salvation. Then comes *trust,* the assurance that what Jesus has done is enough and I can give myself to him. Someone has said, "Faith is born when a felt human need comes face to face with the love of Christ. When we see him as he is our hand gets a grip on it; that's faith." It is like swallowing, which won't keep you alive but enables you to receive what will keep you alive. Faith happens when it happens.

The critical truth here is that it is faith *apart from works.* "By grace you have been saved through faith, and this is not your own doing; it is the gift of God—not the result of works, so that no one may boast."[38] It is the truth which becomes the main thrust of Paul's letter to the Galatians and, incidentally, was the singular doctrinal truth that set Martin Luther to launch the Reformation. I share three formulas that I learned a long time ago to help us define the distinction:

Works = Salvation
Faith + Works = Salvation
Faith = Salvation + Works

The first is basic to every form of non-Christian religion and is embraced by many serious moralists. It is the idea, simplistically told, that God has a big scale into which he piles our good deeds and our bad deeds, and if on the judgment day our good deeds outweigh our bad deeds, he will reward us with blessing. Sadly, the second is held by many Christians, and this is what concerned the Apostle. It is the idea that we must believe in Christ and what he has done redemptively for us, but then we must devote our lives to adding our good deeds and religious acts *in order to please God* and then ultimately be accepted by him. Paul wrote to the Christians in Galatia to warn them of "another gospel" that compromised the true Gospel. The biblical message, the Gospel of the Apostles, is the third formula, namely that we are made right with God, saved, *by faith alone, which in turn issues in our good works. Simply put, the good works are not a condition* for our salvation, but *the consequences of it.*

The formula is not Faith = Salvation, but Faith = Salvation plus

Works. It is by faith alone, but the faith that saves is not alone. Inherent in the faith is the dynamic for the good works. New creations in Christ will produce good works.[39] If there are no good works, then there is question as to the reality of the faith. But the overriding truth is the adequacy of what Christ has done in his redemptive acts to satisfy the claims against us. The Bible declares that Jesus paid it all. What happened at Calvary and at the tomb is so profoundly satisfying that it is arrogant presumption to think that we could add anything more to supplement! How silly it sounds when we try to claim that we believe in Jesus and his death and resurrection—*and* we also took pies to our neighbors in times of sorrow, or we were baptized and regularly attended church, or we even gave up watching television during Lent. Lord, have we done enough to earn your favor?

> Not the labors of my hands
> Can fulfill the law's demands;
> Nothing in my hand I bring,
> Simply to Thy cross I cling.

And what about assurance? When has one produced enough good works or been good enough, either to make it on his own or to add to what Jesus has done? What a blessing to rest in the truth: "Since we are justified by faith, we have peace with God through our Lord Jesus Christ, through whom we have obtained access to this grace in which we stand; and we boast in our hope of sharing the glory of God."[40] Faith is a response to God's matchless favor, acceptance of his gracious bounty. We trust God because we have no other adequate way to express our thanks.

Yes, there are many gospels. There is a social gospel to which all Christians must commit themselves in obedience to our Lord's command to love your neighbor. But there is a GOSPEL which only Jesus Christ can give. Hurting, starving, dying persons need to be assured that Jesus loves them. I learned recently that the following was originally written for a dying child: "Jesus loves me, this I know; For the Bible tells me so." What a tragedy, that the Church is withholding the GOSPEL from the world and the church!

"Q. 1.   What is your only comfort, in life and in death?

A.   That I belong—body and soul, in life and in death—not to myself but to my faithful Savior, Jesus Christ, who at the cost of his own blood has fully paid for all my sins and has completely freed me from the dominion of the devil; that he protects me so well that without the will of my Father in heaven not a hair can fall from head; indeed, that everything must fit his purpose for my salvation.

Therefore, by his Holy Spirit, he also assures me of eternal life, and makes me wholeheartedly willing and ready from now on to live for him.

Q. 2.   How many things must you know that you may live and die in the blessedness of this comfort?

A.   Three. First, the greatness of my sin and wretchedness. Second, how I am freed from all my sins and their wretched consequences. Third, what gratitude I owe to God for such redemption."[41]

7 A Person Just Like Jesus

The Bible talks about one God existing in three Persons. We speak of the Trinity, which means three-in-one. One of these Persons is the Holy Spirit. The King James Bible uses the phrase "Holy Ghost," which causes a problem. "Ghost" conjures up words like eerie, unreal, strange, unusual, and even whimsical. It is often associated with excitement and fear. Thus, guidelines are established to indicate the presence or non-presence of the Holy Spirit in our lives or the life of the Church. If there is no warm feeling in our religious expression, if we are unable to do the unusual or supernatural, if we do not speak in a strange language—these are some of the tests. However, the first thing we learn about the "third Person" is that he is called the "Spirit of truth" (reality).

It would be presumptuous to attempt to define or illustrate the Trinity. We are dealing with an inexhaustible and incomprehensible personality. We cannot begin with an abstract notion of the unity of the three-in-one and then attempt to explain the differences in the persons. The Bible does not talk about a *doctrine* of the Holy Spirit; the word "Trinity" is not a biblical word. Rather, the Bible reveals the truth about a living reality, starting with the witness of the three divine Persons and then beckons us to search out the blessed unity, as an act of faith. The truth about the Holy Spirit is appreciated more through worship than reason.

We are introduced to the Holy Spirit in a spectacular way on the Day of Pentecost.[1] What happened was a once-for-all first-century historical event in which the Holy Spirit ushered in a new era of the Church, and empowered it to fulfill its witness of the Gospel. There were attendant miraculous displays for the infant Church, as there were with the birth of Jesus Christ. The Holy Spirit came in power and blessing in the Old Testament,[2] and effected the virgin birth of Jesus.[3] At Pentecost, he came to enliven the Church.

There are those who plead for a new Pentecost, by which they seem to mean that we need some of the miraculous evidences of the first-century Church. However, the overpowering message that we learn is that the Holy Spirit is a divine Person, and the burden of truth about him is that we, by faith, experience his personhood. To be overly occupied with the gifts and evidences of the unusual in our lives is to miss the blessing of the Holy Spirit. Our greatest need as Christians today is to experience his presence and to live under his guidance, with his power motivating us in every area of our lives.

The Holy Spirit *is* a reality. He is a person; every reference to him in the Bible uses the personal pronoun. If you are a Christian, then you have been born anew "from above" by the Spirit.[4] As a Christian, the Holy Spirit lives with you and is "in you."[5]

The Bible teaches that there are basically two things God wants for his people: to be spiritually satisfied and to give witness to that satisfaction to each other and to the rest of the world. The Holy Spirit is given to us to cause it to happen.

He wants us to be spiritually satisfied. On one of the Hebrew festival days, Jesus, observing the emptiness in the religion of the celebrants, cried out: "Let anyone who is thirsty come to me, and let the one who believes in me drink. As the Scripture has said, 'Out of the believer's heart shall flow rivers of living water.' "; and the recorder adds, "Now he said this about the Spirit, which believers in him were to receive. . . ."[6] It is Jesus Christ who came to fill up the void in our lives and to give us the "abundant life"[7]; it is the Holy Spirit who makes it happen. It is not religion but the Holy Spirit, taking the things of Christ, who can satisfy our restless hearts. Paul prays "that according to the riches of his glory, (the Father) may grant that you may be strengthened in your inner being with power *through his spirit,* and that Christ may dwell in your hearts through faith, as you are being rooted and grounded in love."[8]

The night before Jesus was to be put to death, the disciples spent some blessed time with him. They were in spiritual turmoil. They had been companions of the Lord for three years, hearing his teaching and believing in his mission. They had experienced the excitement and the heartaches of following him, and had always found him faithful. They had given themselves to him and to his cause. Now, with the announcement that he is to leave them, they are confused, disillusioned, fearful, and questioning. Where do we go from here? What about the cause? What will happen to us, and to you? There are some doubts and some anger.

The biblical record tells us that "Jesus knew that his hour had come to depart from this world and go to the Father. Having loved his own who were in the world, he loved them to the end,"[9] and gathered with his disciples for the Passover meal. It was an eventful evening during which he spoke to their needs: "Do not let your hearts be troubled. Believe in God, believe also in me." He assured them of the reality of heaven and that he would return to take them to himself. He told them to pray expectantly and to keep his commandments. Then he announced that his Father would give them *another advocate* to be with them forever: "This is the Spirit of truth . . . You know him, because he abides with you, and he will be in you. I will not leave you orphaned. . . ."[10]

There are three words that stand out in this promise. One is *"orphaned,"* which is an exact translation of the biblical word. Other translations are "comfortless" and "abandoned." In other words, someone would be there with them continually, another person, *just like Jesus.* That is the thrust of the distinguishing Greek word for "another." The disciples would have a constant companion, a Divine One, who would be to them what Jesus had been during the three years in which they followed and trusted him. He would be more than an influence, he would be a person possessing the essence of God and all his attributes. The Holy Spirit would be their *Advocate,* literally one to stand by, to comfort, to plead a cause, to help, to strengthen, to encourage. Very simply, the promise was that the Spirit will satisfy you spiritually, he will be beside you and within you always and he will not leave you comfortless.

Through the years of my ministry, I have heard the testimony of many people who have known the quiet ministry of the Holy Spirit in the time of their greatest need. Paul talks about a "hope that does not disappoint us, because God's love has been poured into our hearts through the Holy Spirit who has been given to us."[11]

The Holy Spirit's satisfying ministry is rich. It is he who gives the confident assurance of our relationship to God. Paul puts it this way: "You did not receive a spirit of slavery to fall back into fear, but you have received a spirit of adoption. When we cry, 'Abba Father!', it is that very Spirit bearing witness with our spirit that we are children of God, and if children, then heirs, heirs of God and joint heirs with Christ."[12]

How do I known that I am a Christian? I just know—somehow I just know! The Holy Spirit gives witness to this testimony: "See what love the Father has given us, that we should be called children of God; and that is what we are!"[13] It is the ministry of the Holy Spirit to interpret in our experience the richness of God's grace given to us in Jesus Christ. Jesus said, "When the Spirit of truth comes, he will guide you into all the truth . . . He will glorify me, because he will take what is mine and declare it to you."[14]

It is interesting that the Holy Spirit's ministry is a self-effacing one. He calls our attention, not to himself, but seems to magnify Christ, the one who by his life, death, and resurrection brought us the grace of God. If you have ever been in Washington, D.C., at night, you may have noticed that the dome of the Capitol building is lighted to show its beauty; but it is interesting to note that you are not conscious of the spotlights enveloping the scene. Your attention is focused on the dome. It is something like that with the Holy Spirit who illuminates Christ.

It was the prayer of the Apostle Paul that God would give to his people a "Spirit of wisdom and revelation" as we come to "fully" know Christ,[15] for it is "Christ himself, in whom are hidden all the treasures of wisdom and knowledge."[16] It is satisfying to know that the Holy Spirit can lead us to explore in depth the vastness of God's grace and to experience the reality of it in our daily lives. Years ago, as a seminary student, I was invited by an elderly minister to share my testimony with a large class of young people preparing for church membership. The class time opened with our singing, "More About Jesus Would I Know," and the best memory I have of that afternoon was watching this pastor, who had had years of blessed experience with God, singing more lustily than any of us. He told me later that there is still much to learn about God's amazing grace. The Holy Spirit is there to teach us.

Many Christians struggle with what has been called "the victorious life." They are discouraged with what Paul describes as the struggle within the Christian between the old nature and the new. "I do not understand my own actions, for I do not do what I want, but I do the very thing I hate."[17] Undoubtedly you know what he is describing. The struggle goes on daily—guilt comes, our lives seem arid, there is no satisfying fruit, I am "wretched," to use Paul's word, who will rescue me from this body of death, the instrument of sin? Listen: "Thanks be to God, through Jesus Christ our Lord!"[18] Then we read of a tremendous promise: "There is therefore now no condemnation for those who are in Christ Jesus. For the law of the *Spirit* of life in Christ Jesus has set you free from the law of sin and of death. For God has done what the law, weakened by the flesh, could not do . . . *so that* the just requirement of the law might be fulfilled in us, who walk not according to the flesh but according to the *Spirit*.[19]

First there is the promise that, though the struggle goes on, God has freed us from judgment—Jesus has taken that for us. Second, the Holy Spirit has brought a new dimension into our spiritual makeup, the *principle of life*, which becomes the dynamic for doing what God wants us to do. Have you ever applied the principle of death to a rose bush by pruning it back, cutting off its branches, sometimes harshly, only to discover within the plant the principle of life, which causes it to recover and produce lovely flowers? Every day of our lives we struggle. The principle of sin and death is always there, but the promise assures us that victory can be ours because the "Spirit of life" works in us and frees us to do God's will.

Furthermore, though the principle of death will one day fell us, the same Holy Spirit will bring us to resurrection: "If the Spirit of him who raised Jesus from the dead dwells in you, he who raised Christ from the dead will give life to your mortal bodies also through his Spirit that dwells in you."[20] The same power present on the first Easter Sunday will be there for your day of resurrection! The Holy Spirit is that power.

The satisfying victorious life is not one in which we are finished with sin and death. The real world in which we live is always there with its temptations, and even if we were able to isolate ourselves from that world we would still not be able to escape the part of our sinful nature that is still with us. The victorious life acknowledges the battle waging within us, is humbled by it and allows it to teach us of our continuous need of grace. It experiences God's ongoing forgiveness and cleansing,[21] and knows that there is a dynamic within not only to effect our salvation but to change our lives—causing us to move in a new and fruitful direction. That is the satisfying work of the Holy Spirit in the sincere Christian.

Then there is the fruit. Paul describes it: "The fruit *of the Spirit* is love, joy, peace, patience, kindness, generosity, faithfulness, gentleness and self-control."[22] The forcefulness of this announcement is that it is in direct contrast to what you can expect from sinful human nature: "Now the works of the flesh are obvious: fornication, impurity, licentiousness, idolatry, sorcery, enmities, strife, jealousy, anger, quarrels, dissentions, factions, envy, drunkenness, carousing, and things like these."[23] Wherever men and women go, sin goes, and sin only goes where men and women go. Nothing we see in the daily news should surprise or shock us. The sincere Christian longs to live on a higher plane, and the Holy Spirit makes that possible because he lives out the character of Jesus in and through us, bearing the fruit described above. "Those who belong to Christ Jesus have crucified the flesh with its passions and desires. If we live by the Spirit, let us also be guided by the Spirit."[24]

Finally, as we begin to discover a relationship with the Holy Spirit and experience his blessings, we learn that there is a certain hitherto unknown freedom. "Where the Spirit of the Lord is, there is freedom,"[25] a liberty that releases us from the limitations of sin and its consequent inhibitions. We are free to be our true self. When the Holy Spirit lives in us, he does not come to obliterate our personality, but to enrich us so that we are what we're supposed to be.

God also wants us to give witness of satisfaction in Christ to each other and to the rest of world. Gathered with his disciples after the resurrection, Jesus said to them: "You will receive power *when the Holy Spirit has come upon you*; and you will be my witnesses in Jerusalem, in all Judea and Samaria, and to the ends of the earth."[26] They had a story to tell! Telling it would make great demands upon them, but it would be good news about Jesus and his love, of how he alone can satisfy the yearnings of the heart. They would have to take their stand for righteousness, truth, and justice. The mission would not be easy, but their resource would be the Holy Spirit, whose power they were to receive.

To be a witness you are required to *say* something, to tell the good news of the Jesus story. The effectiveness of that telling is not found in our human cleverness. Listen to Paul's testimony in writing to the Corinthian Church: "I came to you in weakness and in fear and in much trembling. My speech and my proclamation were not plausible words of wisdom, but with a *demonstration of the Spirit* and of power, so that your faith might rest not on human wisdom but on the power of God."[27] That to a people who thought human knowledge was the key to discovering life's mysteries.

The Bible reminds us that the world does not know God by wisdom but by the truth about Christ's death and resurrection. Some call it foolish that people come to God and find wisdom,[28] but Paul knew it is only the Holy Spirit who can enliven the message. You see, it is not our wisdom that "converts" people. We hold the treasure in earthen vessels, "so that it may be made clear that this extraordinary power belongs to God and does not come from us."[29] Billy Graham knows this well, as does every sincere Christian who has given a simple witness to a friend.

The story must be told, and the encouragement for telling it is the promise of the Holy Spirit. On the day of Pentecost, after Peter's Spirit-blessed message, three thousand people believed. Before a hostile crowd of religious people, Stephen, "a man full of faith and the Holy Spirit," shared the message concerning Christ and was put to death by the leaders. It was the Holy Spirit who directed Philip to witness to the Ethiopian on the road to Gaza, which results in the conversion of the young man.[30]

The secret of sharing our faith with others is not found in our organizing for evangelism, or in our clever arguments or our attractive personalities. In the early Church, as in the Church today, evangelism "happens." The Bible does not offer a program for evangelism. It must be authentic, spontaneous, contagious, and grow by its own inherent grace. The seeking world is not looking for a display of strange phenomena; they are looking for human beings who, like themselves, are faced with all the confusion of life, but who are real, to share the Good News.

What about spiritual gifts? The Bible gives us answers in Paul's first letter to the Corinthian Church.[31] First, they are gifts of *grace*, charismatic. It is strange how the word "charisma" has become the definition for the magnetic personal charm possessed by certain persons; however, in reality the word defines the gifts and talents God bestows upon his people. They are the blessings of grace, which many desire but cannot earn. God allots them just as he chooses.[32]

Secondly, they are gifts *of the Holy Spirit*, the same Spirit who alone enables us to say "Jesus is Lord." Some of the gifts seem to be supernatural in their working, others seem to be natural talents, but all are Spirit-inspired dand are displays of the Spirit. Third, there are varieties of gifts, services, and activities; I have counted at least twenty in three places in the New Testament.[33] They range from forms of leadership and service to the working of miracles. I doubt that the list exhausts the number of gifts God has, or will yet bestow upon his people. The Bible does not indicate that all of the gifts are evident during all eras of church history. God is certainly not limited in equipping Christians by his grace to function effectively in their lives and witness to the Christian community—and beyond.

Fourth, not all Christians are given the same gift. "Each has a particular gift from God, one having one kind and another a different kind."[34] The gifts are allotted by the Spirit, as he chooses, to each individual. Paul uses the figure of the human body to illustrate the place of gifts in the Church. "For just as the body is one and has many members, and all the members of the body, though many, so it is with the church."[35] He then says that just as every part of the body is equally important for the functioning of the body, so the various gifts in the Church have been distributed "for the common good." There is no hierarchy among the gifts. The more spectacular are mingled and balanced by the others. All are so basic to the life and witness of the Christian community that all must be treated with honor.

These words were written to the Corinthian Church because the use of gifts was a problem there. This was a gifted church,[36] but it was a quarreling church and thus was confusing the witness.[37] They had allowed the rivalry of the culture about them to creep in, elevating knowledge above grace, and some were declaring themselves an elite group because they had this gift or that. Sad to say, this has been a problem in the Church through the years. Some consider themselves spiritually superior to their fellow believers. This is the reason that Paul speaks of "a still more excellent way," and shares what has become the classic love chapter in the Bible.[38] Without love permeating the fellowship, the gifts are a "noisy gong or a clanging cymbal," amount to nothing and accomplish nothing. Love is the greatest gift of all.

The purpose of gifts is for the common good. They are meant to equip Christians for the work of ministry and for building up the Church in unity that it might fulfill its mission.[39] Peter adds: "Like good stewards of the manifold grace of God, serve one another with whatever gift each of you has received . . . so that God may be glorified in all things through Jesus Christ. To him belong the glory and the power forever and ever. Amen."[40] The use of our gifts calls for humility and love that is genuine.[41]

This leads to a final observation. The ministry of the Holy Spirit is *in and through the Church.* Therefore, the gifts are not primarily for the individual Christian's satisfaction, but for the sake of the Church and its witness. Paul says: "For in one Spirit we were *all* baptized into one body—Jews or Greeks, slaves or free—and we were *all* made to drink of one Spirit." He then goes on to talk about the various gifts in order that the "body" might function with unity, power, and purpose. The New Testament model of the Spirit-blessed church is one where there is deep hunger for the kind of fellowship which effectively demonstrates the power to establish the right relationship with God, and a common joy in expressing praise and gratitude to God. And from that Spirit-blessed commonality comes the witness that Jesus promised: "By this everyone will know that you are my disciples, if you have love for one another."[42] It was said of the early Christians during their time of persecution: "Behold how they love one another."

The fifth book of the New Testament could be entitled "The Acts of the Holy Spirit," for he was present in and worked out the blessing and will of God through the Church. He is the same Spirit who dwells in God's people today. We need to know and experience him. We need to listen to his testimony concerning God's grace in Jesus Christ. Our hearts and minds should be open to his gracious guidance. We must honor him as we worship the Father and the Son. We are called to "walk in the Spirit" and "to be filled with the Spirit." We must acknowledge his presence within us and the Church, and trust him to be everything that the Bible claims him to be.

> Come, Holy Ghost, our souls inspire
> And lighten with celestial fire.
> Teach us to know the Father, Son,
> And thee, of both, to be but one;
> That through the ages all along
> This, this may be our endless song.

8 Words to Do

Christian behavior springs from an experience of grace. Many of the basic doctrines of our faith come alive as they are worked out in our behavior. For example, the first eleven chapters of Romans give us the most exhaustive truth about God's redemptive purpose as fulfilled in Jesus Christ. Then the twelfth chapter begins: "I appeal to you *therefore . . . by the mercies of God* to present your bodies as a living sacrifice, holy and acceptable to God. . . . Do not be conformed to this world but be transformed by renewing of your minds . . .," followed by a number of practical directions about attitudes and behavior consistent with the knowledge of and faith in the God who has redeemed us. The Bible declares: "Without faith it is impossible to please God," and adds: "Faith without works is dead."

That leads us to think about Christian morality. What is distinctive about it? First, certainly with the Bible as our textbook, we are committed to a biblical morality that comes from God. Peter wrote: "As he who called you is holy, be holy yourselves in all your conduct; for it is written, 'You shall be holy, for I am holy.' "[1] As God behaves so we are to behave, and that calls for something distinctive.

There is a logic to biblical morality. "In the beginning God created the heavens and the earth" is the magnificent theme with which the Bible begins. A universe is brought into being. Behind it all is the almighty Creator-God! He made all things good, thus we live in a universe that has quality about it. There is a purpose, plan, and direction. And there is order—what is created is complete, whole and sound. The word "universe" means "turned into one," suggesting that all creation is a comprehensive whole of all that exists. God made it all and he holds in together and gives it meaning.

The early creation included plants, animals, and things, each made after its kind. Then God created man and woman to be his image-bearers. They were made for relationship with himself and were given dominion over all that he had made. The universe is something to be discovered, enjoyed, shared, and protected. Within this completed creation are structures. The lion has specific qualities making it different from the horse or the elephant, and each is given a name. Lions mate with lions, not zebras. So much of biology, indeed all of science, is discovering the structures. Humans have freedom to explore, *but always within the structures!*

There is an orderliness in every chemistry lab. The structures are our creative possibilities; humans can travel to the moon! The structures are not a prison, but give substance to dreams; they give meter to music and tonal quality to sing it. "Sunrise, Sunset" may sound monotonous, but it is the routine that makes the world go round. There is a natural law, and the horizons within it are limitless. To ignore the order and structures leads to disaster. Atomic power can destroy, the ecology wavers, people starve. H.H. Farmer put it this way: "If you go against the grain of the universe you are going to get splinters."

Just as there are laws and absolutes in the physical world, so there are norms and laws in the area of human relations. The God who created the universe in order made the man and woman to live in harmony within themselves, each other, and the cosmos. They were to be superior to the other forms of life, which exist according to the survival of the fittest and know nothing of the nobility of relationships. As humans, created in God's image, we are in the world with other humans, and with them we discover responsibility, warmth, fulfillment. That is the way it is supposed to be. God has worked a moral law into his created universe. The summary commandments "You shall love the Lord your God" and "You shall love your neighbor as yourself" are foundational. They are the logic for human behavior. To go against the grain of these structures will also lead to getting splinters. The biblical story demonstrates it. God said to the man and woman, "Don't" and they did! Cain killed his brother, Abel, and from there the story unfolds—a record of tragedy detailed in the history of nations.

Fundamental to our knowing the blessing of the moral laws is realizing that it springs from God's essential *loving* quality. Because he loves his image-bearing ones, he wants them to be healthy, sound, happy, and free, so he declares his absolutes. As a loving, caring parent says to her child who is about to place his hand on a hot stove burner, "Don't," so he who made us knows that true freedom is dependent upon limitations and responsibility. His matchless love says, "You shall not. . . ."[2]

Many think that when God says "You shall not commit adultery" he doesn't want us to have any fun. Quite on the contrary, God made us male and female for each other, saying "the two will become one flesh." Within the structure of monogamous marriages this most precious human relationship opens up possibilities and fulfillment beyond measure. Like the violin and the bow when brought together, the man and woman can complete that for which they were made. Out of it comes poetry and music, which express the deepest parts of human relationship. That is what God intended it to be and gave the commandment to protect its intimacy. When people act outside the structures, the tragedies are as fresh as this morning's paper. What happens when humans don't love their neighbor, when they kill and steal, bear false witness, covet, when they don't worship the Lord their God? They become the prodigal a long way from home, far from the love of a Father who wanted so very much for them. And what about the ones sinned against—those exploited, used, profaned, abused, enslaved, ignored—the victims of their prodigal ways? When men and women defy the moral laws inherent in creation, they destroy one another. Society hurts. Perversion degrades the very ideal of human personality.

The commandments were never meant to be an arbitrary set of rules given by a tyrant-god to keep his subjects under control; rather, they are wise and good guidelines for people loved by a loving God. Pious Jews always knew that and found health in living by them. The Torah pointed them in that direction, and so does the New Testament point all of us.

Hence, biblical morality is a protest against the prevailing moral philosophy of our day, called secular humanism. I emphasize "secular" because *classical* humanism, which began to flower toward the close of the Middle Ages, was desperately concerned about the dignity and worth of the human being. The Humanists rightly challenged the Church, which had sublimated the human spirit for centuries by a tyrannical, religious, political authority. Some of the reformers, like John Calvin, shared similar concerns and applauded the enlightenment. Calvin had a passion for intellectual honesty and praised many of the secular writings, seeing in many of them a humanitarian concern for the common man that was absent from the official Church. The leaders of classical humanism were very sincere, intensely so. Their writings were prolific as they worked constantly to find answers to the human situation. They were idealistic, having great confidence in human progress. Out of humanism came the Renaissance, which was marked by the flowering of the arts and literature and the beginning of modern science. The names of DaVinci, Michelangelo, Copernicus, Galileo, and Newton creep up in the history of the time. Much of what we enjoy today we owe to those who allowed the human spirit to soar.

However, the evolution of classical humanism, which began to thrive in America during the early twenties, has shown the tragedies of many of their assumptions. Humanism is defined as a philosophy that asserts the dignity and worth of men and women and their capacity for *self*-realization *through reason* and *rejects supernaturalism*. Largely through the teaching of Rene Descartes, humanism began to eliminate God from the scheme of things and to exalt human reasoning. According to Descartes, knowledge comes wholly from pure reason, without even the aid of the senses. Hence, the universe no longer appears to be a field of divine action but a realm of physical laws that can only be looked at scientifically. The beginning of knowledge is doubt. "How do I know I know?" Answer: "That which I can prove by observation." Reality is what you can touch. Two plus two equals four. You can prove that by placing two apples next to two other apples, and counting them as four.

You cannot prove God, however, so you get rid of any idea about God! But, you see, once you have done that, you erase all indications of the supernatural. There is no reality outside the physical, and even its laws are the result of evolution and not from God. More importantly, you eliminate all the norms and rules of behavior. You are left with the man and woman "in a box" with animals, plants, and things—and other humans who are free to do their own thing. There is no authority outside themselves except REASON. As the humanist manifesto puts it: "There is no substitute—neither faith nor passion." The only reality is in "the box." Humans are reduced to a part of nature and have emerged as a result of a continuing process of development. Biologically, the genes are predictable; sociologically, humans can make the highest culture. They are basically good, but it is the environment that makes them bad. Psychologically, the mind and brain are one, chemically and mechanically motivated. The brain has nerve cells, called neurons, which transmit and receive impulses between one another in continuous interplay. Consciousness is no longer a mystery. The only true reality is the physical place men and women inhabit with animals, plants, and things.

Everything else is subjective. Love is irrational, beauty is only psychological, truth is relative, sex is only physical like other bodily functions. What about responsibility? Humans live with unbridled freedom, adjusted by a kind of "social contract," by vote of the majority, but will change with new circumstances or another generation. There is no censorship, no principle, but success and performance. The only authority is experience after experimentation. Morality is always relative to time and place. Its issue is permissiveness. Human sinfulness is ignored.

It is easy to dismiss all of this as just another philosophy; however, this amoral thrust has worked its way into western culture with such subtlety that we fail to see it as the message of most of current music, drama, art, and literature, as well as in the marketplace. We have a tendency to join in the fun, without seeming to care what it does to the human spirit. But if we really love people, we will recognize its hurt. There is an unknown in the human makeup that strains beyond the physical, reaching for idealism, warmth, feeling, reality, beauty, love—the things that make up the human spirit but are denied by secular humanism. The very thing classical humanism hoped to free has become bondage to an alien philosophy, which denies its existence. It is a "philosophy of despair." Listen to one of its writers: "Man can count on no one but himself; he is alone, abandoned on earth in the midst of his infinite responsibilities, without help, with no other aim than the one he sets himself, with no other destiny than the one he forges for himself on the earth. Death is an overpowering absurdity." So much of the despair comes out in the form of perversion in people's creative expressions. They reach for escapes by humor, drugs, mysticism, romanticism, work, even religion, and especially sex. Each time they get bored, they find another invention in an attempt to leap out of the box.

Christianity is the only true reality. It talks about life and hope. Humans find their real freedom living within the structures. When sin with its alienation intruded, driving us to try to live outside the structures and spelling death, Jesus Christ came. He lived, died, and rose to make it possible to rediscover the blessing of God's will. Within the structures love is love; beauty is beauty; truth is truth; righteousness is righteousness. There is a logic to biblical morality.

We return to the Gospel. The God who ordained the norms and laws as part of creation laments over Jerusalem for the consequences of its waywardness.[3] Then in history's grandest hour, he gave us a Savior. He shows his love for the prodigal, no matter how many of the structures he has violated. He loves the sinner! The very law the wayward has broken shows him his need of a Savior and can lead him home. The profligate, the adulterer, the exploiter, the thief, the murderer, the profaner—all can be forgiven and restored, made whole. The heart of the Gospel is that God forgives sin! "If you, O Lord, should mark iniquities, Lord, who could stand? But there is forgiveness with you, so that you may be revered."[4] God does forgive sin! There is a way back through Jesus Christ.

So how do the "forgiven" behave? The law takes on new meaning; it becomes a lively guide for Christian behavior. The structures are still there. God's grace frees us from the condemnation of the law, but it does not free us from the responsibility to keep that law. Paul was shocked at the very idea of an attitude of license: "What then are we to say? Should we continue in sin in order that grace may abound? By no means! How can we who died to sin go on living in it?"[5] Loving God and loving neighbor are the guide for all Christian behavior. The difference now is that because of the Holy Spirit's sanctifying grace, it is possible to live by these precepts. The ancient commandment is made a new (fresh) commandment,[6] as though it had been tucked away in the cold precepts of the Law of Moses, and is now brought out and clothed in flesh and blood in Jesus Christ. It is given a heart. It is lifted from the dusty archives and made alive in the Christian community.[7]

Listen to Jesus: "Do not think that I have come to abolish the law or the prophets . . . for truly I tell you, until heaven and earth pass away, not one letter, not one stroke of a letter, will pass from the law until all is accomplished," and he issues a warning to those who would teach otherwise. The Christian disciple will live by the rules, *and much more,* for Jesus adds: "I tell you, that unless your righteousness *exceeds* that of the scribes and Pharisees, you will never enter the Kingdom of heaven."[8] What was the righteousness of the Jewish leaders? It was God's law! But they insisted on a legalistic obedience of the law and had worked out in detail what that implied for almost every moment of a person's life. The law had become a straitjacket, a heavy burden placed on those who wanted to please God. Religion was lost in ceremony and the structures had become strictures.

There is more to it than that, said Jesus: "You have heard that it was said to those of ancient times, 'You shall not murder'; and 'whoever murders shall be liable to judgment.' But I say to you that if you are angry with a brother or sister, you will be liable to the judgment; . . . and if you say, 'You fool,' you will be liable to the hell of fire." Whew! That covers the whole arena of human relationships. He goes on: "You have heard that it was said, 'You shall not commit adultery'. But I say to you that everyone who looks at a woman with lust has already committed adultery with her in his heart."[9] That exposes our secret lives—our thoughts, what we read, what we watch, how we talk. No wonder Jesus would say to a bunch of religious bigots about to stone a woman caught in adultery, "Let anyone among you who is without sin be the first to throw a stone at her."[10] Jesus continues: "You have heard that it was said, 'You shall love your neighbor and hate your enemy.' But I say to you, Love your enemies and pray for those who persecute you . . . for if you love those who love you, what reward do you have? Do not even the tax collectors do the same? And if you greet only your brothers and sisters, what more are you doing than others? Do not even the Gentiles do the same?"[11]

Years ago I learned this triad:

> To return evil for good is devilish;
> To return good for good is human;
> To return good for evil is Christian!

Note the distinctive about Christian love. Christian Discipleship leads to excessive righteousness. It goes beyond the letter to the heart of morality, and it is always subject to what James calls "the *royal law* according to the scripture, 'You shall love your neighbor as yourself.' "[12] That brings all the "shall nots" into the positive. Paul says: "The one who loves another has fulfilled the law. The commandments . . . are summed up in this word, 'Love your neighbor as yourself.' Love does no wrong to a neighbor; therefore, love is the fulfilling of the law."[13]

This commandment thrusts Christians into the arena of social responsibility with a new ethic, which is often diametrically opposed to that of the world. It calls for new values, new priorities, new lifestyles, all embraced and motivated by the profound love which the Bible speaks of in the Greek word "agape." The distinctive of biblical morality is that Christians are not called primarily to judge the world's waywardness but to love the world with all the intensity that comes from having, as sinners, experienced the love of God at Calvary.[14]

Follow Jesus in his ministry—his teaching and example. He dined with sinners and scolded the religious separatists for judging him for doing so.[15] He was moved with compassion for the harassed, the helpless and straying multitudes,[16] and exposed the expert in religious law who "wanted to justify himself," by telling the story of the Good Samaritan, who though despised by the Jews showed mercy to his neighbor, while the priest and the Levite passed by on the other side.[17] When Jesus talked about morality, he reserved his sharpest censures for religious people who had so twisted God's law that it had become enslavement to rules and not structures for fulfillment and freedom.[18] And when Jesus talked about morality to his disciples, it was about *being* a certain kind of distinctive person: " . . . poor in spirit . . . those who mourn . . . meek . . . hungering and thirsting after righteousness . . . merciful . . . pure of heart . . . peacemakers,"[19] and he topped it off with the new commandment.

It was LOVE that gave us Calvary, that tempered God's law with grace, that is the fruit of the Spirit, and that "covers a multitude of sins."[20] Biblical morality is a mentality, not jut a code of ethics. It sees fellow humans, not as sinners but as those created by God, bearing his image and dignified by the Incarnation of Christ. It sees them living outside the structures and weeps over their misery. Christian love will be jealous for their personhood. History bears ample witness that those who wish to treat others badly first dehumanize them by pushing them down into a sub-normal, sub-human category. This then gives them the pseudomoral basis for treating them as lower creatures who need to be controlled. It was Hitler's solution to the "Jewish problem." It allowed slavery in our country and exploitation of the native Americans. It is the ruse behind the hate-mongering of our present scene.

The Crusades and the Inquisition of the Middle Ages, the New England witchcraft trials of the seventeenth century were crimes of religious arrogance. The ultimate blasphemy is marching under the banner of the cross in a protest of hate, or burning this symbol of redeeming grace in the yard of a person of color (while hiding behind a white sheet). The current kind of pseudopatriotism, bearing the slogan "born again" and embracing a multitude of social obscenities, is of the same stripe.

When Paul wrote to the Christians in Rome "not to think of yourself more highly than you ought to think, but to think with sober judgment," he revealed the tendency of Christians to think of themselves spiritually and morally above "the rest," and therefore qualified to deal with "the sinner." The Bible says "Let love be genuine—literally "without hypocrisy." We are called to minister love—"to abound in love, walk around in love, provoke one another to love and good deeds, labor in love, extend hospitality to strangers, bless those who persecute you, overcome evil with good." That's "gutsy" love, not the stuff of novels and poetry, nor the sweet talk of religious idealism. It springs from the heart of God, flows through the cross, and becomes the moral fiber of Christian behavior. It will wend its way through the commandments into attitudes and deeds. It will become eventful, as John says: "How does God's love abide in anyone who has the world's goods and sees a brother or sister in need and yet refuses to help? Little children, let us love, not in word or speech, but in truth and action."[21]

No one said that it would be easy to "live" love in what Paul called a "wicked and perverse" culture. There are too may gray areas, particularly in a pluralistic society. It is not a pretty world out there; sin and misery abound; it is messy and sordid sometimes. It is a world of people away from God and under his judgment. But we are called to "shine as stars" in the world.[22] We are to love that world of people where they are, rather than where we think they ought to be. Christians, particularly in America, have a tendency to expect too much from a culture that is caught in the trap of humanism. There is no Christian nation. Some nations have been influenced by Christian principles, and those principles have become foundational in the great documents of our beloved country. America has been singularly blessed because of them. However, the failure to practice those principles comes back to haunt our history, as well as the history of other nations that have been called Christian. The Christian principles, plus a good deal of the "milk of human kindness" and a whole lot of the sovereignty of God, have caused societies to survive; but no amount of Christian idealism can organize or create the ideal society. It is wrong to promote Utopia. Only the gospel of Jesus Christ can regenerate, and we cannot expect unregenerate people to do the will of God, especially when the regenerate have so difficult a time conforming to the ideals. We live in a pluralistic culture, guaranteed by our Constitution. We may be offended by it, but we are called to love its people; and if we really love, then we will grieve over its tragedy. It is the world God loved and sent his son to redeem.

Love means to practice truth. Isaiah, after recounting the sins of God's people, said "Wash yourselves; make yourselves clean; remove the evil of your doing; cease to do evil, *learn to do good;* seek justice, rescue the oppressed."[23] Love requires us to be authentic in our morality; that begins with knowing our own sins. How easy it is to be selective in our causes while denying the subtle sins within us. For example, not all sins are sexual. Many of them are aberrant, and they are abhorrent; however, when the Bible classifies transgressions it isn't selective. It lists sexual sins along with every other kind of wickedness—covetousness, malice, envy, strife, deceit, bitterness, gossip, pride, bragging, disobedience to parents, slander, folly, heartlessness—to name a few,[24] and Jesus said that these all come from the heart. Christians are not immune to the subtlety; so often we are lured into the amoral culture of secular humanism and confuse freedom with license. We often live outside the structures in sexual behavior, in the marketplace, in attitudes toward minorities, the poor, the causes we choose. Our motives are often relative and not always pure. Sometimes we even laugh at their vulgar humor. It is so easy to ignore the blind spots in our own attitudes and rationalize our own behavior. That is why Jesus said "Judge not that you not be judged," and that Paul said "vengeance belongs to God." Hence, learning to do good begins with "washing ourselves clean." That requires intense self-examination leading to confession of all of our sins and then availing ourselves of the cleansing that comes from forgiveness.[25]

There is a piety to the Christian life. It is marked by integrity. Micah called it "walking humbly with your God."[26] If one stays close to Jesus Christ, drawing spiritual life from him, there will be real fruit. Then we are ready to *learn to do good.* And it does take some learning: sorting our motives, working through our subjective prejudices, walking in another's moccasins, knowing the biblical principles—and above all *practicing* love. We learn best by practicing. Every Christian must discover how to "do good" within God's assignment. John said that the world might hate you, because you love so passionately.[27]

Finally, loving the world God loves begins within the Christian community. We need each other in love, and the fellowship is where we best learn "to do."

9 In the World But Not of It

Christians are called to be something special. Echoing Old Testament language concerning Israel, Peter wrote to the Church: "you are a chosen race, a royal priesthood, a holy nation, God's own people, in order that you may proclaim the mighty acts of him who called you out of darkness into his marvelous light."[1] Jesus said that we were like "salt" and "light." Inheriting Israel's responsibility to be a blessing to the world, we have been called to be "holy"—literally "set apart"—for that mission. As defined by the New Testament Greek word, the Church has been "called out from" the rest of mankind to be different; to develop a culture that demonstrates what it means to trust and serve the one living true God, and to mediate his love to a prodigal world.

In the previous chapter, the emphasis was upon what Micah said the Lord required of us—"to do justice and to love kindness."[2] It is our responsibility to love our neighbors as ourselves. However, Micah added that we were "to walk humbly with (our) God." Today there is much discussion about justice and mercy, but little about walking humbly with God. That suggests a personal piety and that scares us. To some it suggests a kind of "oozing synthetic unction," as one seminary student put it in talking about the "Jesus boys" types. One woman said: "My husband is so spiritual I can't stand him."

However, the Bible does teach about a life of godliness, the sincere, mature and faithful experience of Christian men and woman. It is the kind of living that bears a divine impress in all relationships. Paul wrote to young Timothy: "Train yourself in godliness," which is the biblical word for reverence and respect, and also contains the essence of pure goodness. In the Sermon on the Mount, Jesus teaches that the truly blessed are those who are poor in spirit, who empathize with hurting people, who hunger and thirst for righteousness, are merciful, pure of heart, and are ready to suffer for what is right.[3] He says that these people are the most Godlike, true citizens of the Kingdom of God. In a sense, they are not *of* this world and are sometimes called "pilgrims and strangers." One of the Presbyterian forebears spoke of his conversion experience as "when I got my head out of time into eternity," when commenting on Paul's saying that "our citizenship is in heaven,"[4]

Yet to say that Christians are "not of this world" is not to imply that they are otherworldly. In fact, their commitment under God is to be *in* the world. They are called "the light of the world" and the "salt of the earth"; they are to be "blameless and innocent children of God . . . *in the midst of* a crooked and perverse generation in which (they) are to shine like stars in the world."[5]

Christians are not called to be indifferent to the world, retreating to a monastery or spending all of their time in Bible study and prayer. They are to relate to a very real world where people actually live their daily lives. If we are to minister the truth and blessing to the world, then we have got to be in it. Light is only good where there is darkness, and salt is only meaningful where there is something that needs flavoring or preservation. Stars only shine with meaning on a dark night. The Christian seeking spirituality does it within the context of the world around him.

The early Christians discovered their piety while surrounded by the decadent Greek / Roman culture, described as wicked and adulterous. Abraham was called "a friend of God" while settling his family and descendants in the pagan lands of Canaan. David shares the great devotional Psalms, not as a priest, but as a shepherd, soldier, and king. Our Lord himself ministered in a world where "crossed the crowded ways of life" and which eventually put him to death. There is no escapism in Christian discipleship. We are here by the design of the God who redeemed us. Jesus prayed not that the Father would take his disciples out of the world, but that he would protect them from the evil one and then added, "As you have sent me into the world, so have I sent them into the world."[6] We are to be godly people in a sometimes godless world.

That means that the struggle for personal piety is never easy. In the first place, piety in our own lives is difficult to observe, for the moment you do observe it, that very moment you show yourself not to be pious. It is a paradox that the more truly good a Christian becomes, the greater sinner he sees himself to be. In the second place, the world is too much with us. There are televisions, bosses, dishes to wash, computers, flat tires, mortgage payments, peer pressure. We are continually enticed by a modern culture begging us to "keep up with the Joneses," which calls for a lifestyle that requires more money, and shouts for us to be successful. The cry for fun and frolic is always inviting. Then there is the interior warfare of our own soul where there are conflicting claims of self and God. There is the stubborn fact of suffering . . . and the faults of others . . . always something.

The struggle to overcome these forces often leads to a distortion of piety. Jesus warned of practicing our piety before others to be seen of them, and told us not to let our left hand know what the right hand is doing when we make gifts of mercy; he told us not to make long prayers in order to make a good impression.[7] Paul warns against those who urge forms of asceticism, such as forbidding marriage and demanding abstinence from certain food.[8] How easy it is for the forms of religion and self-deprivation to substitute for the real thing. True devotion gives way to religious rites. Holy days and seasons cover a lot of weekday sins. Kierkegaard said of the formal church of the nineteenth century: "They think they are practicing religion, but they are only playing church." Sometimes it is easier to be pious than to be good.

So what does it mean to be spiritual without being phony, without being holier-than-thou or a goody-goody or too "salty"? Paul describes those who are spiritual as "mature" and thus able to discern spiritual things; they are aware of a reality beyond the "natural."[9] I hasten to warn that spirituality is not "spiritism" or "spiritualism," so popular these days in their appeal to those searching for meaning. They teach that all reality is spiritual and that our only resource for living is within ourselves or in the ethereal spirits from out there somewhere as they invade us with messages and mystical power. What they offer is an apparent escape from the real world. In contrast, a spiritual Christian is one who is motivated by the Holy Spirit, a *person*, not a mystical force.

Many sincere Christians seem always to be looking for some new experience, usually ecstatic, or waiting for a special word from God—attending another retreat or revival meeting, discovering the latest technique, reading the newest "how-to" book or pamphlet. In this life-is-so-daily culture, we do need times to be away, alone or with others, for renewal, to review and weigh values, and to give expression of our gratitude to our Lord. Jesus on one occasion said to his disciples who had just returned from a mission and were excitedly telling of their experiences, "Come away to a deserted place by yourselves and rest awhile," for many were coming and going, and they had no leisure even to eat. However, the biblical picture of discipleship is of a confident and relaxed trust in the love of God—a tranquil state of the soul assured of its salvation in Christ. Paul speaks of the "peace of God that surpasses understanding,"[10] and of letting "the peace of Christ rule (our) hearts."[11] This is the Hebrew "shalom," meaning completeness and more than just the end of hostility. Isaiah said, "In returning and rest you shall be saved; in quietness and in trust shall be your strength."[12]

At peace with God, maturing Christians learn to rest in the grace of God, so joyfully sure of the love of God that even during the trials of life they will be sustained. It is a love, measured at Calvary, that now "floods their hearts" and gives them hope.[13] Thus, it is possible to be "spiritual" in our kind of world, a world in which we are to minister God's grace.

Christian piety or spirituality begins with an attitude toward God. The biblical word means loyal devotion and reverence. It embraces a quiet relationship with God, walking humbly with him. The Psalmist put it this way: "As a deer longs for flowing streams, so my soul longs for you, O God."[14] That is deep calling unto deep. He meditates upon him day and night. He desires the person of God, not simply his gifts. The pious one is profoundly respectful, unashamedly worships God, is reflective and contemplative. Paul describes his pursuit of God: "How changed are my ambitions! How I long to know Christ and the power of his resurrection . . . Yet, I do not consider myself to have 'arrived' spiritually, nor do I consider myself already perfect. But I keep going on, grasping ever more firmly that purpose for which he grasped me."[15] There is a certain quality to that kind of commitment. Paul adds: "All of us who are spiritually adult should set ourselves this sort of ambition."

The spiritual Christian will practice the disciplines of prayer, Bible study, worship individually and corporately, and will strive to love God with the whole being. When the heart responds to God's love with emotion, he or she will balance it with faithfulness to God's

Word when seeking his will. He will reach out to fellow Christians for love and friendship in the faith, that together they might explore the richness of God's grace and his will. Together they will become "participants in the divine nature."[16]

There is more, Peter says: "Make every effort to support your faith with goodness, and goodness with knowledge, and knowledge with self-control, and self-control with endurance, and endurance with godliness, and godliness with mutual affections, and mutual affections with love."[17] This describes a quality of personal living, always as part of the fellowship, but personal nonetheless. It involves leading "a life worthy of the Gospel."[18]

In addition to the above qualities are these: humility, gentleness, long-suffering, patience with others, eagerness for maintaining peace within the fellowship, speaking truth and words that build people up rather than those that tear them down, controlling anger, doing away with bitterness, violent outbursts, emotional yelling and contemptuous name calling, being kind, tender hearted, and walking around in the kind of love that marked Jesus' commitment to others.[19] All of these qualities are called graces, and the Greek word for "grace" means "charm, beauty, attractive." Christian piety that is genuine will be something special.

How lovely! Wouldn't it be nice if people would just think nice thoughts. What a wonderful world (or church) it would be if only people were kinder, we say as we go out the church door on a bright Sunday morning. But what can you really expect in this kind of a world? You can't be that good. But wait—the world of the early Christians was far more dismal than our present age, yet these are the qualities that were precisely meant to be the marks of Christians. The Apostle Paul would not be satisfied with anything less than a commitment to try to live these graces. He says, "I beg you to. . . ."[20] That translations does not do justice to the Greek word used, nor do others like "appeal," "beseech," "plead." It can be a call to commitment and actions—let's get on with it.

It is possible to live these graces if one stays close to God, walks humbly with him, and draws on his resources. The Apostle prayed that you "may be filled with the knowledge of God's will in all spiritual wisdom and understanding so that you may lead lives worthy of the Lord, fully pleasing to him, as you bear fruit in every good work and as you grow in the knowledge of God. May you be made strong with all the strength that comes from his glorious power."[21] The resources are there if the commitment is there, for the virtues are the fruit of the Holy Spirit lived out in the Christian's daily life.[22]

It is of particular note that the Scriptures, when talking about piety, single out the virtue of chastity with unusual emphasis. Paul sums it up: "This is the will of God, your sanctification: that you abstain form fornication; that each of you know how to control your own body in holiness and honor, not with lustful passion like the Gentiles (heathen) who do not know God."[23] He goes on: "But fornication and impurity of any kind, or greed, must not be mentioned among you, as is proper among saints. Entirely out of place is obscene, silly and vulgar talk; but instead, let there be thanksgiving" . . . "Put to death, therefore, whatever is earthly: fornication, impurity, passion, evil desire, and greed . . . These are the ways you also once followed, when you were living that life. But now you must get rid of all such things."[24] The Greek words used in these references, and in numerous others, are intense words. The practice of such behavior is associated with "darkness."

Christianity introduced a new virtue into the New Testament world, a pagan world. It elevated human sexuality and womanhood to the highest level. It has been called a moral miracle. Not all sins are sexual, and our society suffers with a multitude of sins of inhumanity; however, perhaps there is nothing that destroys a culture as much as sexual immorality. The pagan world that surrounded God's ancient people, Israel, as well as Christians in the first century, was one that "knew not God." The Book of Leviticus exposes it in a kind of ancient Kinsey report in chapter 21 and elsewhere, and finds YAWE saying to his people: "You shall be holy to me, for I the Lord am holy." The sins were those of raw lewdness. The same was true in the Greco / Roman Empires. The philosophies and religions of that period venerated the passions and the sexual organs. Women were the instruments for men's accommodation, wives were for bearing children and mistresses were for men's pleasure. I recall visiting ancient Ephesus and learning that the brothel was across the street from the library. The temple of Artemis in the ancient city was staffed with hundreds of priestesses who were sacred prostitutes employed in the worship of this goddess of fertility. The tokens of the veneration are still available in the tourist stores in Greece. Promiscuity was alive and well in the ancient cultures. Some have insisted that our modern scene is different. People are more "sexually active" and therefore need to be accommodated. There is nothing new about it; it is as old as the Garden of Eden, when the man and woman discovered that they were naked.[25]

Nothing so degrades the human personality, causes the most innate guilt, or destroys a civilization as does the tragedy of sexual exploitation. I asked a young historian in Greece about what happened to Alexander the Great, who supposedly as a young man wept in his tent because there were no more worlds to conquer. He replied that a nation was lost because most of his army had syphilis. That may not be the sum of it, but perhaps it is emblematic. It is fair to surmise what role the present exposure of screen and literature is playing in a nation gone prodigal and hurting morally. AIDS is taking its physical and spiritual toll, and thousands of youth are learning that there is nothing sacred about the human personality.

The Bible shows us another picture of the sexual encounter. It begins by saying: "Therefore a man leaves his father and his mother and clings to his wife, and they becomes one flesh. And the man and his wife were both naked, and were not ashamed."[26] Jesus restated it to his contemporaries.[27] God made us male and female and to complement each other—"to the pair," as some translate the biblical reference. God equipped the man and woman to mate with each other, and he called it good. What happens between a man and a woman in sexual expression is romantic and good. The chemistry of sex is a wonder. The encounter is the most precious of all human relationships. Nothing is so personal as a person's sexuality, and nothing is so intimate as the linking of two personalities when a man and a woman become "one flesh."

Mating is not limited to humans. Beasts mate—God made them for that, and that is good. However, they do it promiscuously. The male is the aggressor and rounds up his harem for the annual rut, simply for impregnating. There is no commitment to one female; there is no romance, no sharing of souls, no moral element in what they are doing. Animals simply go into heat and have no control over their urge—and certainly no sense of responsibility. Procreation is their only destiny. Hence, to drag down the sexual encounter between two humans, made a little lower than the angels, to the level of bestial behavior is the ultimate insult to the human personality. When sex becomes casual, just another body function like eating or going to the bathroom, or recreational like having a game of tennis, devoid of commitment, it is simply subhuman and evil, going against the design for humanness.

God's plan was for something better. Human sexuality has to do with persons, not simply bodies. It distinguishes between a person and a thing. You cannot love the body without loving the heart of a person. Further, God planned for humans to mate face-to-face, totally exposing the two personalities in an intimacy never found in any other human relationship. The last barrier is removed in the marriage bed. The door is opened wide for the fullest emotional expression and satisfaction—and with an awesome freedom. It is human love at its height. It is personal; it is intimate, delicately so. That is why rape and sexual abuse and aberration are so evil, and why to cheapen and vulgarize this gift of God's creative love is so obscene.

Nowhere does the Bible call "sin" the beauty or the sexual ability of the human body, nor the emotions that pulsate the body. It only says, "You shall not commit adultery," which means that sex is so precious, so intimate, that its experience is confined to one man and one woman, totally committed body and soul to each other in holy marriage. It is reserved for the intimate place; it is not something for stage and screen. Peter Marshall used to remind young people that sex is like a gardenia—not just any flower—but a gardenia, which in addition to being sweet, is white and stands for purity. But still more significant is the quality of the gardenia which we call delicate; a gardenia can be marred by the least careless touch. And then he would express the hope that young people might so live that their pathway, which leads to the marriage altar and beyond, might be fragrant with the scent of untouched gardenias. Virginity, though not popular and oftentimes ridiculed, is still very precious.

Agape (New Testament love) is the ruling guide in the whole of sexual behavior. Passion can be creative or destructive. Selfless love devoted to the welfare of the other sees sex not simply as a moral issue, but as a person issue. Agape elevates passion, indeed fulfills it. It will not exploit simply for selfish satisfaction. True love reaches for intimacy and finds it in an authentic sexual encounter. Christian piety will reach for that, even in our "enlightened age." "Having sex," even "safe sex," is never an end in itself.

There is caution: A marriage contract does not guarantee the kind of fulfillment the Bible talks about. In fact, there are many marriages that are denials of God's design. Sex can be a method of expressing things other than love: domination, boredom, lust, pride, hatred, chauvinism. The very fact that it is so enjoyable is a temptation to use it selfishly rather than dedicate it to each other.

I close this lengthy section with the biblical word: "Shun fornication!" Every sin that a person commits is outside the body; but the fornicator sins against the body itself. Or do you not know that your body is a temple of the Holy Spirit within you, which you have from God, and that you are not your own? For you were bought with a price; therefore glorify God in your body."[28] Christians are neither animal nor pagan!

Paul's parting word on spirituality: "Finally, beloved, whatever is true, whatever is honorable, whatever is just, whatever is pure, whatever is pleasing, whatever is commendable, if there is any excellence and if there is anything worthy of praise, think about these things."[29] Practice godliness.

I can hear some readers reacting: " Is there no joy in the Kingdom? The Christian life doesn't sound like fun." To be sure, the Church has often given that impression with its legalisms and false piety. However, the Bible overflows with expressions of rejoicing, being glad, and expressions of contentment: "Rejoice with an indescribable glorious joy" . . . "Rejoice in the Lord always; again I will say, Rejoice." Indeed, there are many more such expressions. In the Old Testament, there are at least a dozen Hebrew words to describe it: "to leap," "cry aloud," "laugh," "play," "be glad." There is joy abounding in God's design for his people, but it is a distinctive joy.

First of all, joy is never an end in itself. Many confuse joy with "pleasure." Pleasure is a good word meaning "that which pleases and delights." But when it becomes an end in itself, it degenerates into indulgence, giving oneself over to it, or dissipation, called "hedonism" in the Bible; it is casting morals to the wind as a way of life. It tells of the prodigal, living with abandonment, always running around in search of something more titillating, when the excitement of the previous adventure has run its course. So often it is at the expense of others. Paul describes the one who lives that way as "dead even while she lives."[30]

Secondly, the Bible interprets "joy" as "satisfaction." The New Testament words for "rejoice" and "joy" come from the same root as "grace," meaning that which gives satisfaction. Pleasure is a by-product rather than an end in itself. I am captivated by the expression concerning Jesus, the "pioneer and perfecter of our faith, who *for the sake of the joy* that was set before him endured the cross"[31] It must have been the satisfaction that he had finished what he had come to earth to do as mankind's Redeemer. The other word that describes it is "happiness" or contentment. It is never at the mercy of circumstances, but something that is deep and abiding, going back to the Beatitudes [32] which describe the "happy ones." (The word "blessed" means happy.) They know the satisfaction of gaining victory over self, of being sensitive to the needs of others, doing acts of mercy and the right thing, even if it means persecution, of having been instrumental in bringing reconciliation between parties. There is also the satisfaction (joy) in helping someone find the way home spiritually, being forgiven for a wrong done or forgiving another, wiping the slate clean for new beginnings. All of this describes a joy that comes from living where roots run deep. Happy are those who "are like trees planted by streams of water, which yield their fruit in its season, and their leaves do not wither. In all they do they prosper."[33]

Thirdly, this kind of joy is in response to experiences of God's grace and goodness. The Psalmists sings: "Happy are those whose transgression is forgiven . . . and in whose spirit there is no deceit." The joy of sins forgiven! There is the happiness that comes from the knowledge of God's presence and provision, of the hope one has in Christ, both for tomorrow and eternity, of belonging to God and his family, of answered prayer, the loveliness of a sunset and of "all things bright and beautiful." There is joy of the "harvest."

What about the thrill of victory? When my team won, when I conquered the computer, wrote a poem, built a cabinet, made an honest business deal, built a brick wall, got good grades in school, broke a habit. What about the joy when good things happen? The birth of a baby, a happy marriage and marital sex, of finding something lost, good news from a friend, the hug of a child. Then there is the joyous freedom of not having to look over my shoulder to see who may be watching, of innocence. These are some of the things that result in what Peter calls "unspeakable joy."

Walking humbly with one's God is the satisfying life, and in no way does it lack. You *can* be in the world, yet not of it, and still have fun!

"Pursue peace with everyone, and the holiness without which no one will see the Lord."[34]

10 Through the Church

There are two overriding themes that stand out in the heart of the Gospel: God loved the world so much that he gave his Son to redeem it, and Christ loved the Church so much that he gave himself up for her. And for both, God's love cost the death of Jesus Christ and placed a tremendous estimate upon the world and the Church. In Chapter VI we considered the Good News for the world. Now, let us consider God's love for the Church.

In the Book of Revelation we are given a picture of the glorified Christ walking among the churches. He knows all about them as they go through hard times, suffer from persecution, and attempt to remain true. As their Lord he is seen commending them, encouraging, comforting, warning, correcting, *because he loves them* and *he knows their destiny* in God's purpose for history. The Church must be the Church.[1]

We first learn about the Church when Jesus says to his disciples, "On this rock I will build my church."[2] This announcement came after Peter affirmed that Jesus was "the Christ, the Son of the living God." It would be the confession by which the company of Jesus' people would henceforth be known, and it is the confession of the Church today.

The Church came into being on the day of Pentecost, when the small company of disciples plus some others were gathered in one place. Suddenly the Holy Spirit burst upon them. Peter preached a Spirit-blessed sermon, and the response was so great that three thousand people were baptized into the Church. This was followed by the Lord adding to their number day by day 'those who were being saved.'[3] From that time onward the Church became God's instrument for blessing mankind, and the Apostles began to emphasize its central place in God's purpose. The Church became God's special people.

In Old Testament history Israel was God's unique blessed people, but now the focus is changed. By the redemptive work of Jesus Christ, God has brought into being a new entity made up of Gentiles and Jews. Both have access to the Father, both are fellow heirs, members of the same body, and share the promise of the Gospel. Paul speaks of the "household of God, built upon the foundation of the apostles and prophets, with Christ Jesus himself as the cornerstone."[4] This is something new. For centuries the Jews had hoarded God's truth, thinking the Gospel was meant only for them. But a miracle happened, the middle wall between Jew and Gentile was broken down, and *in Christ* there would no longer be Jew or Gentile. For that matter, there would "no longer be slave or free . . . no longer male and female; for all . . . are one in Jesus Christ."[5] There is no other reconciled and reconciling fellowship like it in all of history. It is called THE CHURCH OF THE LIVING GOD!

Paul, the Apostle of the Church, shares amazing truth about the Church. After humbly accepting his responsibility as an Apostle he says, "This grace was given to me to bring to the Gentiles (nations) the news of the boundless riches of Christ, and to make everyone see what is the plan of the mystery hidden for ages in God who created all things; so that *through the church* the wisdom of God in its rich variety might now be made known to the rulers and authorities in the heavenly places. This was in accordance with the eternal purpose that he has carried out in Christ Jesus our Lord."[6] Can you see the exclamation points that should follow the announcement *through the church?*

It is as though a great drama, which began with creation, is being played out on the stage of history—the drama of redemption—and all heaven is looking on. On the stage, the Church, possessing the unsearchable riches of Jesus Christ, is front and center. What a thrill to be a part of that—and what a responsibility! The Church is God's gift to the world.

When Paul speaks of the *manifold* wisdom of God, he uses a Greek word meaning "varicolored" or "many-faceted." Perhaps in a school physics lab you experimented with passing a beam of white light through a prism and discovered the phenomenon called refraction by which the light is diffused or spread out in such a way that you can see its component colors—the spectrum of the rainbow: red, orange, yellow, green, blue, indigo, violet. Scientists tell us of the many subtle shades and blendings of colors and of ultraviolet and infrared, not discernible to the human eye.

Thus, Paul uses the word *manifold* to describe the wisdom of God found in the riches of Christ. God declares himself in a person, and that person is Jesus in whom are hidden all the treasures of wisdom and knowledge.[7] In a sense, the Church is the prism, and God refracts his varied forms of truth through it! We are told that God has a purpose and "plan for the fullness of time, to gather up all things in (Christ), things in heaven and things on earth. In Christ *we* have also obtained an inheritance, having been destined according to the purpose of him who accomplishes all things according to his counsel and will."[8] The Church is right there in the center of things!

So what is the Church? The word comes from the Greek *ecclesia*, meaning an assembly, a group of people brought together for a special purpose. It literally means "called out from." Another word, from which we get "synagogue" or "congregation," speaks of people who gather together. The first word, however, sometimes used in military sense, carries the idea of people who are "summoned" for a particular purpose. It reminds us of a people chosen or picked out, a theme occurring over and over again in the Old and New Testaments.[9] The Church has a commission from her Lord.

The Church is made up of people who have a common destiny. They have been blessed, redeemed, forgiven, made members of God's select family. They have known the favor of God in a singular way and share a common identity. They have a common confession and a common mission: to be a blessing to the world. As noted in an earlier chapter, that mission is primarily threefold: to demonstrate before the world what it means to trust and serve the one, true, living God; to be the receivers of the Word of God and to share it with the world; and to mediate Jesus Christ to the World—that is, help them experience his grace and love.

In theology, *ecclesiology* is the study of the Church. It appears to be one of the most neglected doctrines of our day because so much emphasis is being placed on individualized religion. It has caused what someone describes as a new breed of religious window-shoppers and shoplifters. Among so many church "floaters" there is no sense of commitment to a fellowship, no sense of history, no feel for the persecution and trials that the Church has suffered through the centuries. Disgruntled believers oftentimes get together to form a "new" fellowship of like-minded folk and call it the true church, as though Martin Luther, Augustine, John Calvin never lived. The Church, however, has been a phenomenon of almost two thousand years, and its predecessor, Israel, for a lot more years than that. Neither the people of Israel, nor the First Century Church, had the luxury of choosing. In Corinth, for example, there was only one church, good or bad. On Saturday, the daily paper did not list the array of "church opportunities" that we see each week.

The biblical picture of the *ecclesia* is a fellowship of committed people who found their roots in history and their future in heaven. They spoke of the "communion of the saints" and were convinced it included all believers in Jesus Christ—and even those who had "died in the faith."

We cannot deny that the Church has clouded its witness. We do need to distinguish between the Church and organized religion. It is easy for the Church to lose its integrity in *ecclesiasticism*, which means a strong attachment to rituals, traditions, and customs, and the local church becomes mainly the place where you go for special days, for baptisms, weddings, and funerals. Or it may include the Church being ecclesiastically organized in order to accomplish something that may not always be a biblical mandate. Have you noticed how the Church seems to spend so much time in search of an image and mission, and an inordinate amount of time and effort juggling church budgets and playing with symbols rather than getting on with its true calling: to witness and minister in the name of Christ. It is scary when one thinks of the tremendous amount of resources, human and financial, that are spent in church housekeeping, while so much of the time passing by on the other side of the road the spiritual and human tragedies of life.

The Bible shares little about church organization. It was quite simple. In the early days of the church, when widows were being neglected in the distribution of food, seven deacons were set apart for serving their needs and others that arose later. Then elders or overseers were set apart to "keep watch ... over the whole flock ... to shepherd the church of God ... to take care of and manage the church."[10] The Apostles evidently had a special authority in the city of Jerusalem and reviewed what was happening as the Church spread to other lands.[11] But that's about it.

To be sure, today we are the Twentieth Century and not the New

Testament church, and our developmental history is lengthy. The Church has had to deal with complications of its exposure and to adapt to phenomenal growth. Now there is more than caring for widows. The Church has had to adjust to persecution, government tyranny, corrupt religious authority, the Dark Ages, competing philosophies. Its history has given us a Reformation and the martyrdom of human lives. Denominations have arisen in the struggle, and there is the plain fact of geography which contributed to the formation of scattered fellowships when travel was by horseback and boat. In our day, the Church in America is found in a pluralistic society guaranteed by the separation of church and state. Hence, corporations of believers must be formed, and that requires trustees; there are licenses to be secured and all kinds of forms must be filed. Church organization is a must and no longer simple. Yet, somehow throughout a spotted history, God's Church has been there, and evidently God has never deserted it, even in the worst of times. Though he may not have approved of all that the Church has been and done, he has never been indifferent to it.

But organization is not in itself the problem of the Church. It is when the Church turns inward, becomes ingrown, protecting itself and becoming self-perpetuating—when ecclesiasticism sets in and becomes "organized religion"—that it loses its integrity. However, when true to itself the Church is not really an organization but an *organism*. The Church has been biblically described as the flock of Christ, the household of faith, the family of God, the habitation of God, a virgin espoused to Christ, a bride adorned for her husband. But Paul's favorite expression is "the body of Christ."[12] The Church must be organized with order and discipline, but it is more than that. Like the human body it is a composite unity, which is the opposite of individualism. "One body," says Paul, with the head, Jesus Christ; and one life, pulsating and motivating, the Holy Spirit. The expression speaks of sharing gifts and love, of suffering and rejoicing together, of living and moving to accomplish a common mission. A minister friend of mine said that when pronouncing the benediction on a Sunday morning, he envisioned his congregation going out on a Monday to five hundred different fields of occupations as ministering members of the body of Christ, and he was asking God to give each of them and the Body his blessing.

Finally, the Church is neither a movement nor a crusade. It is a *fellowship*, doing what is inherent in a common experience of salvation. No sooner does a person come to Christ, having discovered his love, than he or she begins to reach out for others who have discovered it too. John says, "If we walk in the light, as (God) himself is in the light, we have fellowship with one another."[13] This is something special, and that leads us to the *local* church. Theologians talk of the "invisible Church," which refers to God's redeemed ones in an eternal reference—believers of the past, present, and future. The Bible speaks of a "great crowd of witnesses" surrounding the Church.[14] They also talk of the "visible Church." Our sense of the Church comes not through vibrations of the saints who have gone before, or from an eerie feeling of souls floating around in the atmosphere and bumping into us now and then. Our sense of the Church comes through an assembly where two or more individuals share the same faith and life—where there is flesh and blood and heart.

When Jesus spoke of building his Church, he certainly had in mind the Church at Ephesus, at Corinth, Jerusalem, Rome, First Church downtown and Grundy Center. I have "experienced" the Church in at least fifteen countries and in more than that many different cultures. Sometimes I did not understand their language, but when we gathered around the Communion table, the Church was always there. One must be in a local church in order to know the fellowship. The new and fresh thing the Apostle Paul had to share in the first century world of alienation, and which has been a blessing that spilled over into succeeding centuries, was a fellowship of reconciled people. Some years ago, in the South Sudan, I fellowshipped with Christians from five different tribes, who, before they came to Christ, maintained, at best, a hostile distance from each other. Now they were "one in Christ." The Christian fellowship is a very precious thing. Dietrich Bonhoeffer wrote from his prison cell that the fellowship is too little recognized and enjoyed by those who have the gift every day. When he was deprived of the Church he wrote: 'It is not simply to be taken for granted that the Christian has the privilege of living among Christians. . . . It is by the grace of God that a congregation is permitted to gather visibly in the world to share God's Word and Sacrament . . . the sick, the imprisoned, the scattered lonely, the proclaimers of the Gospel in heathen lands stand alone.'[15]

It is a priceless privilege to have the right to break in upon God, to take our problems, our loneliness, our sorrow, and our joys directly to him. That is exactly the right Jesus gives us in regard to God. There is no need for sacrifice, nor ritual, nor priest. Jesus Christ channels us directly to God for his mercy and grace.[16] The barrier is down. Add to that the fact that the barrier is also down between two or more Christians, and you discover a second precious privilege. That is why the Apostle placed so much emphasis on discovering and cultivating the fellowship: "Make every effort to maintain the unity of the Spirit in the bond of peace."[17] No Christian can survive spiritually very long without Christian fellowship in a local congregation. It is there for you to receive blessing, to remember as in the Lord's Supper; for worship, for encouragement, for experiencing forgiveness, for maturing, for creating a godly culture—and for ministry. The electronic church cannot offer anything like that, and a Christian not committed to a local church will never know the blessing nor the challenge of being part of a people of destiny.

Honest Christians who look at history with clear perception are often embarrassed when they have to admit the dark side of the Church. It is all there to see. The Church has often been a stumbling block in the way of those who seek God as well as having given ammunition aplenty for her gainsayers. Yet, as one historian put it, "The Church is an anvil that has worn out many a hammer." It is difficult to think of any benefit for mankind that did not find its seeds in the Church's Gospel: hospitals, education, social service, beneficent governments. The Church has influenced and structured cultures that civilizations have desperately sought. Even the unbelieving world uses her symbols and her language. Though sometimes only a remnant of the true Church, God continues to bless *through the Church*. The Bible affirms the Church.

11 Hope Springs Eternal

Hope has always been a mark of God's biblical people. The story of hope can be traced from the time of Noah, who believed God and saw his rainbow in the clouds, clear through to those who believed the "word of God and the testimony of Jesus" given John on the island of Patmos.[1]

Sadly, hope is not a distinctive mark of our present generations, which have been described as people afflicted with the sickness of despair. Paul spoke of those who were without Christ "having no hope and without God in the world."[2] It is alarming to see the number of young people whose dreams are shattered and hopes are buried, and those, burdened with life, for whom hope dies before it is born. When there is "un-hope," frustration, defeat, pessimism, cynicism naturally flow, which in turn leads to irresponsibility, carelessness, and too often tragically to suicide.

The Christian Church has a strong "word of hope" for our world, as well as for its own people. The word itself takes on its real substance in biblical language. It is described by at least nine words in Hebrew and one in Greek, and comes through as joyful expectation, confidence, waiting patiently, leaning on, trust, firmness, feeling secure, and even "to flee for refuge." The Bible indicates that hope is no less one of the abiding virtues than faith and love, and without hope the other two are meaningless.

In biblical language, hope is not so much defined as described in the experience of God's people; it comes alive among them. First we discover that hope is founded on the promise of God. Paul speaks of the promise made to Abraham that he would be the father of many nations, and uniquely of the people of Israel. This promise was made when Abraham was quite elderly, and Sarah, his wife, beyond childbearing age. Yet on that promise alone and "hoping against hope, he believed that he would become the 'father of many nations' according to what was said. . . ."[3] Without the promise of God there is no hope, but with it we are assured of all the possibilities of God's eternal purpose. The individual Christian can dream, and the Church can be sure of its destiny.

Next, we must know that both the promise and the hope are based on the person of God, a person whose integrity, power, and love assure the fulfillment of the promise and the expectation. Paul blesses us by saying "May the God of hope fill you with all joy and peace in believing, so that you may abound in hope by the power of the Holy Spirit."[4] Peter speaks of having your faith and hope set *on God*. And the Psalmist often praised by using words like "For you, O Lord, are my *hope*, my *trust*, O Lord, from my youth."[5] God is recognized as the author of hope and promise. It all depends upon him: faithful Creator, Redeemer, Sustainer, whose word cannot fail.

Thirdly, hope is made possible by the redeeming work of Jesus Christ. It was because of his death and resurrection that the future was made possible to those who believe in him. He set us free from the hold of sin. The context of every promise in the New Testament is the redeeming work of Jesus Christ. It was because of this that Paul and others went about declaring the promise of God, and were willing to stand strong in persecution. After Pentecost, the Apostles shared the good news of the death and resurrection, and Paul gave his defense before King Agrippa, saying "It is for *this hope* that . . . I am accused." He went on to define it by saying "that the Messiah must suffer, and that, by being the first to rise from the dead, he would proclaim light both to our people and to the Gentiles."[6]

Hope is born of faith. We often speak of Hebrews 11 as the great "faith chapter" of the Bible, as it tells the record of the Old Testament saints who are spoken of as those who "died in faith (faith-fashion, as one of my professors put it) without having received the promises, but from a distance they saw and greeted them."[7] The chapter could also be called the "hope chapter." It begins: "Now faith means putting full confidence in the things we hope for, it means being certain of things we cannot see."

Fourthly, biblical hope is matured by circumstances. We read: "Therefore, since we are justified by faith, we have peace with God through our Lord Jesus Christ . . . and not only that, but we also boast in our sufferings, knowing that suffering produces endurance, and endurance produces character, and *character produces hope. . . .*" There is no satisfying or complete answer to the problem of suffering, but the Bible deals with it head on—recognizing it is as very real and Christians can go through everything unbelievers experience—cancer, polio, car wrecks, the whole gamut of human hurting. But blessed is that Christian who, having access to the grace of God, knows the ministry of suffering in his or her life. Instead of seeing themselves as victims, or wallowing in acquiescence, they learn patience and how it produces character and the ability to overcome. The Greek word for character literally means "proof," used of metals and coins made valuable in the process of refining fire, which gets rid of the dross and alloys and produces what is genuine.

A Christian is a novice without experiencing suffering. As a pastor, how often I have felt like an amateur when attempting to minister to a dear Christian saint who has gone through so much. Many times I have come away ministered to, when I have learned of the depth of character and maturity, and a hope that can only be known by those who have stood the test. Paul adds: "this is a hope which will never disappoint us," because through the experience we discover that "God's love has been poured into our hearts." In a sense we are shut up to faith when there is no other place to turn, and turning to God we come to know his love that was measured at the Cross, where "while we were sinners, Christ died for us." We can be hopeful in the presence of that kind of love. Christian hope is not simply a doctrine; it is an experience of grace. Read it again![18]

Finally, biblical hope issues in trust and patience. It was true of Abraham who went on hoping when to hope sounded impossible. He waited and trusted God. The same can be said about all the "people of faith" recorded in the Bible. As the Apostle put it: "Now hope that is seen is not hope . . . But if we hope for that which we see not, we wait for it with patience."[9]

"To summarize: There is more here than a "feeling that what is wanted will happen," or a "desire accompanied with expectation" (dictionary), echoed in the expression, "I hope so." The word persists in our daily vocabulary and literature, but often it is simply wistfulness or vague yearnings. Sometimes it is a desire that something ill might happen to an enemy. But hope comes alive among

God's people, because they have a sure part in the future and the purpose of God.

For what do they hope? First, it is evident in the promise of Jesus: "In my Father's house are many dwelling places. If it were not so, would I have told you that I go to prepare a place for you?"[10] It is the positive answer given to the age-old question, "If mortals die will they live again?" As with the problem of suffering, the Bible meets death head on. Our tendency is to push the idea of death to the back of our consciousness so that life can go on as though death did not exist. We have funeral *parlors* and *slumber* rooms, and our loved ones "pass away." There are those who accept death in a sort of stoical, philosophical attitude: Humans die; so what, so do butterflies, flowers, and animals. Death is the "eternal void" into which all life passes. Others defy death—like a moth flying into a flame—I can handle it. They make jokes about it. Some of my most difficult attempts at ministry through the years have been when called by a loved one to visit a family member who was about to die, only to find a rejection of anything hopeful.

There is only one adventure in life as great as being born, and that is dying. Death is the great event after birth. Name them: graduation, marriage, honors, retirement, acts of heroism; they cannot measure up to the great climax, the event that casts its shadow over all of them, indeed over all of life. It comes as a thief stealing from the rich their riches, stripping the strong of their strength, tearing away the mask of beauty, and so on—and then the crisis. The Bible describes the earthly life span as a vapor, a sleep, "seventy years, or perhaps eighty, if we are strong; even then their span is only toil and trouble; they are soon gone, and we fly away."[11] Paul declares candidly: "If for this life only we have hoped in Christ, we are of all people most to be pitied."[12]

Each of us has "a rendezvous with death at some disputed barricade," as Alan Seeger's poem says. And if this earthly life is all there is, why not live it up like the hedonists; why not "eat and drink, for tomorrow you die?"[13] But the Christian Gospel talks about a *"living* hope through the resurrection of Jesus Christ from the dead."[14] Paul adds: "We do not want you to be uninformed, brothers and sisters, about those who have died, so that you may not grieve as others do who have no hope."[15] The Bible declares that there is a true home for the soul, and though people may scoff about the idea of a heaven, Jesus spoke plainly and triumphantly about it. The grave is not the end nor the answer. A whole dimension of life is yet to be experienced by those whose hope is in Jesus.

It is called "our hope of sharing the glory of God,"[16] and "the hope of eternal life that God, who never lies, promised before the ages began."[17] Peter describes it as an "inheritance that is imperishable, undefiled and unfading, kept in heaven for you."[18] We are told that only eternity itself can "show the immeasurable riches of his grace."[19] What this means for the Christian is that the unknown is beyond our human comprehension, which makes the expectance more exciting. "For now we see in a mirror dimly, but then we will see face . . . then I will know fully."[20] One day the Christian will receive a transformed body like the resurrected body of Christ—a "spiritual body"; then he will be able to comprehend and to share in God's glory. We will be made for heaven. Dr. Addison Leitch used the illustration of an older teenager attempting to explain to his ten-year old brother what it is like to love his girl friend. To the brother it makes no sense at all. But let two or three years go by, and the boy puts on a new body; then he begins to understand, he is equipped for the larger experience.

What will heaven be like? The Bible speaks of it as a full, completed salvation: "at home with the Lord." Paul spoke of "departing to be with Christ," and John said "we shall be like him." The Book of Revelation gives us glimpses of the glory, the majesty, and magnificence of God and the splendor that surrounds him, but they come to us in visionary form, which enriches our anticipation but cannot now be fully understood. We learn that it is an existence that never ends and an experience with quality to it. It is *"sharing the glory of God,"* not just sitting around playing harps. I am not sure we should go further in talking about heaven. It would probably mar our expectation!

The point I am making is: *there is something more!* It is the hope of all the promises of redemption fulfilled, and it is that hope that most impacts our lives in the here and now. At the close of the great resurrection chapter, the Apostles says: "Thanks be to God, who gives us the victory through our Lord Jesus Christ. *Therefore,* my beloved, be steadfast, unmoveable, always excelling in the work of the Lord, because you know that in the Lord your labor is not in vain."[22] When we are able to see through the shadow, then we are ready to die. but more significantly for us now, we are *ready to live.* Here is the testimony of a woman who struggled with the inevitable, death from cancer. She came to know the love of God in Christ and the hope of eternal life. "I discovered that until I was free to die, I was not free to live. I would now live by his will and I would die by his will, but because I was free now to rely on his will even in my own death, I was now free to live abundantly." Here is the testimony of all who know that the "sting of death is gone," the last burden is lifted and LIFE takes on its fullest reality. This hope brings all of life into focus. Weighing our values in the white radiance of eternity adds an intrinsic quality to everyday living. Paul encourages young Timothy: "take hold of eternal life," grasp it for all that it is worth, and he gave his own testimony: "The time of my departure has come. I have fought the good fight, I have finished the race. I have kept the faith."[23] If anyone lived life "to the hilt," Paul did. Whether he was sailing rough seas, being beaten with rods, standing before rulers, preaching the Gospel in Athens, languishing in a cruel jail, or mending tents, he lived with eternity's values in view. His ultimate word: "For me, living is Christ, and dying is gain." There is no greater assurance about the Christian hope and what it should mean to every Christian.

This kind of hope puts content into our daily lives. We have spoken of life being "so daily." So much intrudes, and sometimes our prospects seem so helpless. In the Peanuts cartoon, Linus says "Life is so difficult, isn't it Charlie Brown?" "Yes, it is," Charlie Brown replies. Linus continues, "but I've developed a new philosophy—I only dread one day at a time." This seems to be about all we can handle, and Jesus told us to live one day at a time; "Today's trouble is enough for today."[24] He also told us in the same verse "do not worry about tomorrow," which follows a long paragraph where he speaks of "your heavenly Father" who feeds and clothes those who lay up treasures in heaven and strive first for the Kingdom of God. Biblical hope enables us to creatively handle all of life. The promise is "We know that all things work together for good for those who love God, who are called according to his purpose"; and goes on, "Who will separate us from the love of Christ? Will hardship, or distress, or persecution, or famine, or nakedness, or peril, or sword? . . . No, in all these things we are more than conquerors through him who loved us."[25] This kind of hope fills up life with meaning and anticipation. The Christian is always a realist. Daily life is there—but so is hope!

When Paul says your labor *for the Lord* is not in vain, he introduces us to another dimension of hope. He might well have been called "the Apostle of the purpose of God," because he knew that his work and ours is a part of something bigger. He seems always to be involving the commitment of our lives in a central theme about God's "plan for the fullness of time, to gather up all things in him, things in heaven and things on earth." He says: "In Christ *we* have obtained an inheritance, having been destined according to (his) purpose . . . so that *we*, who were the first to set our hope in Christ, might live to the praise of his glory."[26] Paul knew that the future was always in the hands of God, that history was going somewhere, and that Christians have a part in that developing history. Scripture declares that God's purpose is a thread that ties all history together, that there is a reason to it, and that it will be fulfilled one day. Within the sweep of it are found all the details of *our* lives; they work together for good, precisely because the details are part of a larger whole. Paul states that *our* destiny is part of "the hope of our calling," and tells us to lead lives worthy of this calling.[27] The life to be lived within the purpose of God is something larger than life!

> Only one life, twill soon be past;
> Only what's done for Christ will last.

That puts it in perspective, and it *will* last! That is the message of hope that ties it all together: God fulfills his purpose through his people and promises them a part in the triumphant outcome.

We began with the truth that the Bible tells a story: Creation, the entrance of sin with its awful consequences, the promise of redemption, its unfolding through Israel, the event of Jesus Christ, his death and resurrection, Pentecost and its gift of the Holy Spirit, the Church entrusted with an awesome mission. All of this "while we wait for the blessed hope and the manifestation of the glory of our great God and Savior, Jesus Christ."[28] The story will build toward a summation when the Savior who once came in humiliation comes again in glory as Lord of Lords and King of Kings! It signals the time when "creation itself will be set free from the bondage of decay and will obtain the freedom of the glory of the children of God."[29] In the Phillips translation of the Bible we read that the whole creation is "on tiptoe" waiting to see this wonderful sight. It will be the time when those who are "heirs of Christ" will enter into their inheritance. The final dream is of a universe set free from sin's awful hold.

The Book of Revelation is full of vivid and symbolic imagery, giving us a picture of a throne, living creatures and angels worshipping and singing loud songs, crystal seas, brilliant colors, streets of gold, the sounding of signaling trumpets—all indicating magnificent glory. One of the visions John shares is described thus: "After this I looked, and there was a great multitude that no one could count, from every nation, from all tribes and peoples and languages, standing before the throne and before the Lamb, robed in white, with palm branches in their hands. They cried out in a loud voice, saying, 'Salvation belongs to our God who is seated on the throne, and to the Lamb!' " The multitude are joined by angels and living creatures in the chorus singing

> "Amen! Blessing and glory and wisdom
> and thanksgiving and honor
> and power and might
> be to our God forever and ever!
> Amen."[30]

It is a chorus of praise of spirits set free in the full reality of redemption.

A final scene begins: "Then I saw a new heaven and a new earth; for the first heaven and the first earth had passed away, and the sea was no more. And I saw the holy city, the new Jerusalem, coming down out of heaven from God, prepared as a bride adorned for her husband. And I heard a loud voice from the throne saying,

> 'See, the home of God is among mortals.
> He will dwell with them as their God;
> they will be his peoples,
> and God himself will be with them;
> he will wipe every tear from their eyes.
> Death will be no more;
> mourning and crying and pain will be no more,
> for the first things have passed away.' "[31]

"Words to live and do" erupt in the theme "Hope Springs Eternal."

Hallelujah! Amen!

References

Introduction

1. John 20: 30,31
2. I John 5: 13
3. Colossians 2: 6,7
4. Jude 1: 3

Chapter I

1. II Timothy 3: 16,17
2. Augsburgh Publishing House
3. Romans 1: 20
4. Psalms 19: 1
5. Hebrews 1:1–3
6. Ephesians 4: 11,12
7. Ephesians 1: 17
8. I Corinthians 2: 9–13
9. Romans 1: 16
10. Psalms 19: 7,8
11. Psalms 19: 1
12. Isaiah 11: 6
13. Luke 15: 11ff
14. Luke 15: 1–3
15. Proverbs 8: 22
16. I Corinthians 7:25ff
17. Psalms 119: 97

Chapter II

1. Genesis 1: 27
2. Titus 2: 1,11,12
3. Romans 12: 1ff
4. I John 4: 9–11
5. Exodus 20: 1ff
6. Matthew 18: 3
7. Mark 12: 42,43
8. *Christianity Today* 7 / 22 / 91

Chapter III

1. Genesis 12: 1–3
2. II Corinthians 1: 19,20 (J.B. Phillips Translation)
3. John 20: 31
4. I Peter 2: 9

Chapter IV

1. I Thessalonians 1: 9
12. Exodus 15: 2,11

2. Acts 17: 22–28
3. Jeremiah 10: 3–6
4. Isaiah 40: 18,19; 28–31
5. Hebrews 11: 6 (King James Version)
6. Exodus 3: 13–16
7. Psalms 23: 1
8. Psalms 42: 1,2
9. Psalms 104: 24ff
10. Ephesians 1: 10,11
11. Ephesians 1: 11,12
13. Isaiah 6: 3
14. Isaiah 46: 5
15. Leviticus 11: 44
16. I Peter 1: 14,15
17. Isaiah 6: 5
18. Job 42: 6
19. Isaiah 57: 15
20. Deuteronomy 6: 4,5
21. Romans 1: 21–32
22. Psalms 103: 1–5

Chapter V

1. I John 1: 1
2. Galatians 4: 4
3. Luke 2: 40
4. Luke 2: 52
5. Mark 1: 11
6. H.H. Farmer
7. John 1: 1–3,14
8. Colossians 1: 15–20
9. Colossians 2: 9
10. Hebrews 1: 1–3
11. John 14: 8,9
12. John 1: 18
13. Psalms 32: 5
14. Romans 5: 8
15. I John 4: 9–10
16. Matthew 1: 23
17. Hebrews 4: 14–16
18. Hebrews 10: 10
19. I Peter 2: 24
20. Hebrews 10: 5
21. Luke 3: 35
22. Matthew 27: 46
23. Galatians 3: 13
24. II Corinthians 5: 21
25. Philippians 2: 6–8
26. II Corinthians 5: 19
27. Acts 9: 4,5
28. II Corinthians 5: 17,18
29. Matthew 1: 21
30. Galatians 5: 22,23
31. Matthew 25: 40
32. Helmut Thielicke
33. Philippians 2: 9–11
34. Luke 23: 42,43
35. Acts 8: 35
36. Acts 1: 11
37. Matthew 17: 1–3
38. Revelation 5: 11–14
39. Revelation 11: 15
40. Hebrews 3: 1

Chapter VI

1. Luke 4: 18
2. Isaiah 61: 1
3. I Peter 1: 3–5
4. Romans 1: 1
5. Galatians 1: 11–24
6. Philippians 1: 12–14
7. Acts 20: 24
22. Psalms 89: 14
23. Amos 5: 24
24. Romans 3: 19
25. Romans 1: 20
26. Romans 3: 20
27. I John 1: 8,10
28. Psalms 103: 12

8. Galatians 1: 3–11
9. Galatians 5: 16–26
10. Romans 1: 1–4
11. Romans 1: 16
12. Romans 3: 23
13. Romans 1: 20,32
14. Romans 2: 1
15. Romans 2: 25–29
16. Romans 3: 9–18
17. Romans 7: 17–20
18. Mark 7: 21–23
19. Romans 6: 23
20. Romans 1: 24,26,28
21. Romans 1: 18

29. Psalms 32: 1 (Living Bible)
30. John 8: 34
31. Matthew 20: 28
32. Galatians 3: 13
33. Titus 2: 14
34. Galatians 4: 6,7
35. Ephesians 3: 7
36. Romans 5: 6–8
37. Romans 10: 17
38. Ephesians 2: 8,9
39. II Corinthians 5: 17
40. Romans 5: 1,2
41. The Heidelberg Catechism

Chapter VII

1. Acts 2: 1–13
2. I Samuel 10: 6
3. Matthew 1: 18
4. John 3: 1–6
5. John 14: 17
6. John 7: 37–39
7. John 10: 10
8. Ephesians 3: 14–17
9. John 13: 1,2
10. John 14: 16–18
11. Romans 5: 5
12. Romans 8: 15–17
13. I John 3: 1
14. John 16: 13,14
15. Ephesians 1: 16,17
16. Colossians 2: 3
17. Romans 7: 15
18. Romans 7: 24,25
19. Romans 8: 1–4
20. Romans 8: 11
21. I John 5: 8,9

22. Galatians 5: 22,23
23. Galatians 5: 19–21
24. Galatians 5: 24–26
25. II Corinthians 3: 17
26. Acts 1: 8
27. I Corinthians 2: 3–5
28. I Corinthians 1: 18–25
29. II Corinthians 4: 7,8
30. Acts 8: 29–39
31. I Corinthians 12: 1–31
32. I Corinthians 12: 11
33. Romans 12: 6–8; Ephesians 4: 11; I Corinthians 12: 8–10,28
34. I Corinthians 7: 7
35. I Corinthians 12: 12
36. I Corinthians 1: 7
37. I Corinthians 1: 11–12
38. I Corinthians 12: 31–13: 1–13
39. Ephesians 4: 11–16
40. I Peter 4: 1–11
41. Romans 12: 3–9a
42. John 13: 35

Chapter VIII

1. I Peter 1: 15,16

15. Matthew 9: 10–13

2. Exodus 20: 1–17
3. Matthew 23: 37–38
4. Psalms 130: 3,4
5. Romans 6: 1,2
6. John 13: 34
7. I John 2: 7,8
8. Matthew 5: 17–20
9. Matthew 5: 21,22,27,28
10. John 8: 7
11. Matthew 5: 43–48
12. James 2: 8
13. Romans 13: 8–10
14. I John 4: 9–11
16. Matthew 9: 35,36
17. Luke 10: 25–37
18. Matthew 23: 1–36
19. Matthew 5: 1–10
20. I Peter 4: 8
21. I John 3: 17,18
22. Philippians 2: 15
23. Isaiah 1: 16,17
24. Romans 1: 28–31; Mark 7: 21–23
25. I John 1: 8–10
26. Micah 6: 8
27. I John 3: 13,14

Chapter IX

1. I Peter 2: 9
2. Micah 6: 8
3. Matthew 5: 1–11
4. Philippians 3: 20
5. Philippians 2: 15
6. John 17: 15–18
7. Matthew 6: 1–6
8. I Timothy 4: 3
9. I Corinthians 2: 6–14
10. Philippians 4: 7
11. Colossians 3: 15
12. Isaiah 30: 15
13. Romans 5: 1–10
14. Psalms 42: 1
15. Philippians 3: 10–15 (Phillips Translation)
16. II Peter 1: 4
17. II Peter 1: 5–7
18. Philippians 1: 27a
19. Ephesians 4: 1–3,24–5: 1; Colossians 3: 1–17
20. Romans 12: 1
21. Colossians 1: 9–11
22. Galatians 5: 22,23
23. I Thessalonians 4: 3–5
24. Ephesians 5: 3,4; Colossians 3: 5–8
25. Genesis 3: 7
26. Genesis 2: 24,25
27. Matthew 19: 4–6
28. I Corinthians 6: 18–20
29. Philippians 4: 8
30. I Timothy 5: 6
31. Hebrews 12: 2
32. Matthew 5: 10
33. Psalms 1: 3
34. Hebrews 12: 14

Chapter X

1. Revelation 1: 9–3: 22
2. Matthew 16: 18
3. Acts 2: 47
4. Ephesians 2: 13–22
5. Galatians 3: 28
6. Ephesians 3: 8–11
10. Acts 20: 17,28
11. Acts 15
12. I Corinthians 12: 12–31
13. I John 1: 7
14. Hebrews 12: 1
15. "Life Together"

7. Colossians 2: 3
8. I Ephesians 1: 10,11
9. I Peter 2: 9; Ephesians 1: 4,5

16. Hebrews 4: 14–16
17. Ephesians 4: 3

Chapter XI

1. Revelation 1: 9
2. Ephesians 2: 12
3. Romans 4: 18
4. Romans 15: 13
5. Psalms 71: 5
6. Acts 26: 7,23
7. Hebrews 11: 13
8. Romans 5: 1–11
9. Romans 8: 24,25
10. John 14: 2
11. Psalms 90: 10
12. I Corinthians 15: 19
13. I Corinthians 15: 32
14. I Peter 1: 3
15. I Thessalonians 4: 13
16. Romans 5: 2

17. Titus 1: 2
18. I Peter 1: 4
19. Ephesians 2: 7
20. I Corinthians 13: 12
21. Philippians 3: 21
22. I Corinthians 15: 57,58
23. II Timothy 4: 6,7
24. Matthew 6: 34
25. Romans 8: 35,37
26. Ephesians 1: 10–12
27. Ephesians 4: 1ff
28. Titus 2: 13
29. Romans 8: 19–22
30. Revelation 7: 9–12
31. Revelation 21: 1–4